> e-mail trouble

CONSTRUCTS   The Constructs Series examines the ways in which the things we make change both our world and how we understand it. Authors in the series explore the constructive nature of the human artifact and the imagination and reflection that bring it into being.

Series Editors: H. Randolph Swearer
Robert Mugerauer
Vivian Sobchack

> e-mail trouble

love and addiction @ the matrix

s. paige baty

university of texas press ⟡ austin

First edition, 1999

Requests for permission to reproduce material from this work
should be sent to Permissions, University of Texas Press, Box
7819, Austin, TX 78713-7819.

♾The paper used in this publication meets the minimum
requirements of American National Standard for Information
Sciences—Permanence of Paper for Printed Library Materials,
ANSI Z39.48-1984.

Library of Congress Cataloging-in-Publication Data

Baty, S. Paige, 1961–
    e-mail trouble : love and addiction @ the matrix / S. Paige Baty.
      p.   cm. — (Constructs)
    ISBN 0-292-70863-7 (alk. paper)
    ISBN 0-292-78064-5 (pbk. : alk. paper)
    1. Electronic mail messages—Psychological aspects.
2. Baty, S. Paige, 1961– —Correspondence.   3. Internet
addiction.   4. Human-computer interaction.   5. Love—
Computer network resources.   6. Friendship—Computer
network resources.   I. Title.   II. Series.

HQ1178 IN PROCESS
808'.042'07—ddc21   98-8963

This book is dedicated to Vivian Sobchack.

I thank her for all she has taught me with her courage,
insight, dignity, and humor.

Paige Baty dedicated this book to me, but it stands more
accurately as her commemoration. My friend and colleague
died in July 1997, and this now posthumous work, read in
hindsight, resonates deeply with the force and fierceness
of her life. Resurrected through her words, her spirit again
touched all of us as we completed the final editing of this
book: Laurel, her loving and loyal sister, and Carolyn Wylie
and Jim Burr at the University of Texas Press.

*—**Vivian Sobchack***

Acknowledgments

I would like to deeply thank my sister Laurel Baty for all of the work she has done on this manuscript. She has helped me in more ways than I am able to enumerate. I would also like to thank Scott Stanek for help and technical advice. Leslie Fellows, who makes up a large part of this story, has been a constant companion in my life. I salute her for her joy and love of life. Thank you, Adam Margulies, for everything you've taught me from the apple to downsizing. I am grateful for your support and friendship. I also thank Kirsten Hudson who remains a true friend, always giving of her love in the correspondence that is our friendship. Thank you, Mark Rigby, for always being there. I would like to thank Dr. Deana Jung Prescott for guiding me in the next steps of my journey. Thank you, Jack Schaar. Thank you, Hayden White, for your continued support. I would like to thank all of the editors who have worked on this project. I thank Ali Hossaini for his work on earlier versions of the text. I thank Jim Burr for his continued work in this project. I also strongly thank Carolyn Cates Wylie for help as managing editor and Jean Lee Cole for the book design. Finally, thank you once more, Vivian. The extensive editorial work you performed on this project cannot be overstated. Without you, this book would not be here.

—P. B.

**A Postmodern
Dialogic Exercise
in Learning about
Platonic Love**

or:

**A Computer Geek
Tragedy**

EPIGRAPH ONE:

I need a friend who will never visit yet never leave me.
—*Justin Smith, unpublished poem*

EPISTLE TOO:

And cannot pleasures, while they last,
Be actual unless, when past
They leave us shuddering and aghast,
With anguish smarting?
And cannot friends be firm and fast,
And yet bear parting?

Farewell, dear friend, and when we meet
In desert waste or crowded street,
Perhaps before the week shall fleet,
Perhaps to-morrow
I trust to find *your* heart the seat
Of wasting sorrow.
—*Lewis Carroll, "A Valentine"*

Hi. I'm Paige and I'm an addict. This is the true story of how I got into e-mail trouble over the Internet that links us together in an ever smaller global village. This is the story of how I became addicted to e-mail; how I sent thirty or more e-mails a day, and received as many messages back. I will tell how the noun Hunter S. Thompson became for me an adjective, describing a mild flirtation with desire that ended in apocalypse. The whole thing was, in short, very Hunter S. But this is my story and I tell it with no small amount of trepidation. Read this in the tradition of confessional narrative; think of Augustine, Rousseau, Rimbaud, Burroughs, Barthes, Kerouac, and Kierkegaard (the man who loved pseudonyms as I much as I loved e-mail nicknames and "fingers"). But remember, I am a woman fessing up to how I got tangled up in the Internet, tangled up in ruse and deception. Here, e-mail trouble is female trouble.

Date: Fri., 17 Feb. 1995 22:42:02 CST
To: S. Paige.Baty@williams.edu
From: Neal Sembre
Subject: Dr. Rocket?

HI. I'm assuming that this is Paige's account, and not that of
some under graduate. There's a big jazzfest down here in late
April/early May. Some, as of yet undetermined number, of my
friends are coming to visit for the second weekend so it could
be an intense time. There's always room on the floor if you've
got a sleeping bag or something. So lemme know if you're Paige
(and if so, give me some way of knowing that it's you) and if
you're interested. Looking forward to hearing back from you.
Yours, Neal.

I am circling in on my subject. My subject is the matrix and myself. I want to understand what got me caught. I want to know what
happened to the person I was before I got hooked on e-mail. And
finally in this mourning work, I want to say good-bye to all of those
people I was caught up with, so I can begin another journey. Journeys are stories. This story does not have a clear beginning and end,
but it does have a subject and a trip. Its subject is the matrix, its
treatment the talking cure, a talking tour. I am trying to understand
what moved me through my journey on the information superhighway, what drove me "on the road." Mine is a different trip from
Jack's. We're both dharma bums, but by the time I started traveling
there was less movement on railway cars and buses: people had
begun to move through virtual space. There is no conductor on this
train. Here you travel at the terminal. Still, Jack and I have a lot in
common: we are both crazy Catholic mystics bleeding to know the
world as word. In the beginning was the word, and the word seemed
good. I'm no longer sure it is. These are the confessions of a hungry
artist. These are confessions that take place in utter perplexity at
what it was that moved me to do what I did. I set about writing
myself anew. I decided to make my life an open book. A power
book.

Note: All pseudonyms
have been changed
or invented to respect
the innocent; and the
e-mail inserts are
edited or invented
by the receiver and
author of these dead
letters . . .
Paige maker.

I wasn't just tangled and caught up in a word game. I was stuck in the electronic womb. I was suffocating in the matrix, and no amount of kicking got me out. I had to wait for the water to break in New Orleans. I had to be washed out in a flood of Biblical proportions. I had to be reminded that I lived in a body, and that same body would one day die, and that no amount of storytelling would stop the process. I had to experience death to get back to life. This did not happen just once, but again and again. Remember this while you read: this story is about repetition compulsions. The act of telling the story is yet one more repetition. Each repetition changes the story. Many versions of this story have been lost, and you are reading what remains of what I thought I lived and learned at Williams.edu. This is my account.

```
Date:     Tue, 20 Aug 1996 19:36:45 EDT
To:       williams.edu
From:     @williams.edu
Subject:  IMPORTANT virus situation update PLEASE READ
```

Williams network users,

We are in a disaster recovery situation. The best way that I can describe this is that we are the victims of terrorism. It is as if someone had fired a stinger missile through the front door of Jesup
and it had exploded in the computer room.

This is where we stand: We have been able to recover from our own backups
all user data and files up to 4-August. We have updated our virus scanner to recognize the new virus and have scanned all the restored files
to verify that the system is clean.
If you detect the virus on your PC, the infected file will need to be deleted. An attempt to disinfect your disk could trigger the virus and damage your system.

We strongly advise you, once the system is made available again, to
make backups of your important files to floppy disk. A good way to
do it is to maintain three sets of diskettes and rotate them. In other

words back up to one, next time back up to a second and so forth until

you start over again with the first set. That way if one diskette goes

bad you have a fall-back position. This is what we do here and is why

we are able to restore any data at all now.

As stated at the beginning of this missive: this is a disaster recovery

situation. Jesup support staff will be extremely busy helping users

deal with this situation. Please be patient with us when you call in with a problem. Your problem is important to us and we will get back

to you as soon as we possibly can.

E-mail trouble. As a woman who reproduces in unconventional ways, I had no idea what form my conception would take. Would an angel whisper in my ear and speak the seed of God into my matrix? What ugly creature slouched towards my computer screen to be born? It was born of woman, collaborating with man and god on the Internet. How can I bear what I have borne—and become? This birth did not take place away in a manger, but right at the desk where I was then spending the greater part of my days and youth. Perhaps this is the route of e-mail trouble.

Routes and roots sit at the core of this story. Male routes, mail routes, biographical roots, roots of words, and routes of the letter. This is the story of a route *i* took that got *me* into e-mail trouble, that got me lost in the matrix. I've suffered versions of e-mail trouble all of my life. In sum: my sentence is the period. I bleed a lot, and have since I was a child. Blood-letting go, and bloodlines holding on. I have endometriosis. It changes the way I live in the world. It marks me as a woman again and again. It refuses to be ignored. It also makes it either difficult or impossible to "conceive." It sometimes means having laparoscopies in which the excess endometrial tissue is removed by cauterization. They burn the excesses of your womanhood from you. They tell you it won't hurt too much or too long afterwards. They give you drugs that induce early menopause; they put you on "the pill." There is very little more that can be done for endometriosis short of a hysterectomy, or oophorectomy, or getting pregnant. Getting pregnant helps, because you stop bleeding for nine months. I was advised to get pregnant early. I ignored that advice.

matrix . . . *Pl.* matrixes, matrices . . . in *late L.* womb, in older *Latin* pregnant animal, female animal used for breeding; app. f. *mater* mother, by change of the ending into the suffix of fem. agent-nouns. Cf. matrice. . . .

1. The uterus or womb. Also occas. used for <u>ovary</u>, esp. with reference to oviparous animals.

> **1526** Tindale *Luke* ii. 23 Every man chylde that fyrst openeth the matrix shalbe called holy to the lorde.

> **1547** Boorde *Brev. Health* iii. 8 Abhorsion . . maye come by ventositie and lubricite of humours in the matryx.

> **1615** Crooke *Body of Man* 272 The partes of the Female are the wombe and the rest which by a general name are called matrices. . . .

> **1726–31** Tindal *Rapin's Hist. Eng.* (1743) II. xvii. 74 *note*, The women that attended about Queen Mary alledged that her Matrix was consumed. . . .

> **1803** *Med. Jrnl.* IX. 57 The matrix . . was uncommonly small, and the right ovarium . . had attached to it small excrescences. . . .

> **1840** *Cuvier's Anim. Kingd.* 40 The foetus, immediately after conception, descends . . into the matrix.[1]

My mother and the matrix. The matrix is a cave and a womb (Plato's convoluted hyphen). The matrix I was caught in was man-made. NO OVARIES. Now an artificial life was born from that same womb, a life all about hidden chips and umbilical chords of memory and loss that had to be cut, and reconstructed, and sometimes crashed, and were a lot of times about pain. But the matrix was also about comfort. In the matrix I did not have to live in my body. In the matrix I could be whoever I wanted to be. In the matrix I could travel across time and space and just be some words on a page. I am that blank Paige who wrote herself in the matrix and danced—like the dazzled Madame BOVARY—into disaster. Maybe I wanted to spring—full-blown—from the head of this crazy Mother Zeus. Maybe I thought I'd become immortal if I stayed in the womb long enough.

1. This and following definitions are from the *Oxford English Dictionary*, 2d ed., computer database (1986), s.v. "matrix."

Maybe I didn't want to be in a womb at all, but just found myself there trying to get out. Maybe I didn't know where I wanted to be. I cannot tell you for certain anymore, but I know I loved the ease with which I could move around there and always end up in the same place. I reproduced without any messy pregnancies: I simply cloned simulations of myself and then I played the roles I had scripted for awhile. After a time the roles became too much. I longed to return to a place that felt more like home.

But where was home? Home is supposed to be where the heart is. It is certainly not where the cursor is, but beyond that blinking light in the window, that electronic hearth, I wasn't sure where else I could go. I guess I wanted community, but the ones I loved had pretty much all gone their separate ways. We all lived in the United States but we were always apart. I wanted a grounded community, but there was none to be had. Wendell Berry has said that "because a community is, by definition, *placed*, its success cannot be divided from the success of its place, its natural setting and surroundings: its soils, forests, grasslands, plants and animals, water, light, and air. The two economies, the natural and the human, support each other; each is the other's hope of a durable and a livable life."[2] There was no ground under williams.edu. It was no place for community.

2.

a. A place or medium in which something is 'bred', produced or developed.

> **1555** Eden *Decades* . . .141 They found certaine pearles coommynge foorthe of their matreces. . . .

> **1641** French *Distill.* v. (1651) 161 Untill they . . be received into certain matrixes in the earth which may make them put forth this potentiall saltnesse into act. . . .

> **1727–52** Chambers *Cycl.* s.v., The earth is the matrix wherein seeds sprout. . . .

> **1879** H. George *Progr. & Pov*; x. ii. (1881) 453 This is the matrix in which mind unfolds. . . .

b. A place or point of origin and growth.

> **1605** Camden *Rem.* (1637) 56 The old German tongue, which undoubtedly is the matrix and mother of our English.

2. Wendell Berry, "Does Community Have a Value?" in *Home Economics: Fourteen Essays* (San Francisco: North Point Press, 1987), p. 192.

1867 Manning *Eng. & Christendom* 242 The root and matrix of the Catholic Church.

1896 *Peterson Mag.* VI. 263/1 The matrix of the anti-war feeling was in New England.

c. The formative part of the animal organ. . . .

1854 Owen *Skel. & Teeth* in *Circ. Sci., Organ. Nat.* I. 280 The matrix of certain teeth does not give rise . . to the germ of a second tooth. . .

d. *Bot.* The body on which a fungus or a lichen grows. . . .

1874 Cooke *Fungi* 25 These spores . . deposit themselves . . on the surface of the . . . matrix.

e. 'The inward, soft, pithy and spungy part of any Tree or Plant' (Phillips, ed. Kersey, 1706).

1693 tr. *Blancard's Phys. Dict.* (ed. 2), *Matrix,* . . Among Vegetables it signifies the Marrow or Heart of a Plant.

In the natural setting and surroundings of my body, fungus and lichen grew, spores deposited themselves, and inward, soft, pithy, spongy parts of myself created a community of sorts, a tissue of truth that made me bleed inside. Outside, the wooded and spongy medium of New England seemed beautiful, but remote. The community there seemed embedded in a tissue of lies. Its "natural settings and surroundings: its soils, forests, grasslands, plants and animals, water, light and air" did not support me, seemed cold and hard as rock. I retreated into the womb.

3.

a. An embedding or enclosing mass; esp. the rock-mass surrounding or adhering to things embedded in the earth. . . .

1756–7 tr. *Keysler's Trav.* (1760) I. 48 In the matrix of an emerald, you may see how this gem concretes. . . .

b. *Biol.* The substance situated between animal or vegetable cells. . . .

1881 Mivart *Cat* 17 The structureless substance and fibres form what is called the matrix of the tissue. . . .

1896 *Allbutt's Syst. Med.* I. 115 The intercellular matrix undergoes modifications or degenerative changes during inflammation.

The matrix undergoes modifications and degenerates when inflamed. Something is burning in the matrix. It has a virus, a computer virus, an intercellular virus. Electrical synapses spark thought and desire into wild fires. The matrix is inflamed with words. People send e-mail to one another and sometimes they think they have found community, communion, or fallen in love. When I lived (and loved) @williams.edu. I thought that maybe I could be @home. I found out that my home was not at that address.

4.

a. A mould in which something is cast or shaped; in *Type-founding*, a piece of metal (usually copper) on which the letter has been stamped in intaglio by means of a punch, so that it forms a mould for the face of the type; in *Coining*, the stamp and 'bed' used for striking coins; in *Stereotyping*, the paper squeeze of a form of type, serving as a mould for a type-metal cast. . . .

> **1709** Tanner 3 Oct. in *Ballard MSS*. IV. 53 They find the want of Matrices at their Press. . . .

> **1859** Sala *Gas-light & D*; ii. 27 His nimble fingers are shaping out the matrix of a monstrous human face, for a pantomimic mask. . . .

b. *Antiq.* The bed or hollowed place in a slab in which a monumental brass is fixed.

The place was beautiful in certain ways. I could sit in my study and look at the same mountain that Melville looked at when he wrote *Moby Dick*. I could think about Ethan Frome—the man and the book—because his life seemed so similar to mine. At williams.edu, simultaneously in New England and on the world wide web of the matrix, I could be anyone I wanted to be, could coin myself. In the matrix the letter is sent *intaglio*. Intelligence is spent. Words and history compress into a coin which has lost its value: we send each other junk mail. We face our type: the type. We laser print as we bleed. The matrix is a holy foundry, a founding of hype. Will we be healed? Annealed? Annulled? Is this monumental brass? Or are my nimble fingers shaping a monstrous mask?

I wasn't used to living the way I did @williams.edu. I was used to big mountains, loud sunshine, lots of people, poppies on the mountainsides, and being around a history I had known most or all of my life. When I moved to Williams.edu I left everything that I was used to behind, the very mould in which I had been cast and shaped. I felt a great sadness and longing, but I did not know how to express it. And so I set about trying to live through my days and nights as if I were in a *real* community. The thing with the community I found and lost myself in was that it was never the face-to-face New England village I thought it would be. Paradoxically, it was in an actual New England village that virtual reality became much more real to me than the many interactions of my daily life. Maybe when places are too close and small it is easier to deal with projections, simulations, and phantasms, and it was for this reason that so many of us suffered from the Winter sickness. People drew into themselves, or often spoke about subjects not related to themselves. We played "Who's Afraid of Virginia Woolf?" Conversations were often made up of games. Rarely did we talk about our feelings, our work, and our lives. Maybe everyone was afraid. Everyone was cold. Really facing each other might have meant facing ourselves, something that seemed so often to be an impossibility. I began to know the meaning of being alone in a crowd, only in this case I knew all the other people. That made the loneliness worse. There seemed great holes in my life, great gaping cavities without feeling and talk that needed filling. Maybe it would be easier, I thought, if the crowd were invisible or nameless. And so there was e-mail. I went for the quick fix: the cure. I turned to the salvation doctor many fear and hate and deny and rationalize away, but I thought I needed what was being prescribed. I hoped to fill the gaps in my numbed mouth with something more filling.

5. *Dentistry*. A plate of metal or composition to serve as a temporary wall for a cavity of a tooth during filling.

> **1883** G. Cunningham in *Dental Record* III. 458 No matter whether one or two or even all the walls of the cavity are gone, they may be restored by a matrix.

STEP TWO:
Believe that a power greater than you can restore you to sanity.

THE JUDGE-PENITENT INTERVENES

But I am letting myself go! I am pleading a case! Forgive me. Habit, monsieur, vocation, also the desire to make you fully understand this city, and the heart of things! For we are at the heart of things here. Have you noticed that Amsterdam's concentric canals resemble the circles of hell? The middle-class hell, of course, peopled with bad dreams. When one comes from the outside, as one gradually goes through these circles, life—and hence its crimes—becomes denser, darker. Here, we are in the last circle.[3]

I am circling in on my account, concentrically, eccentrically. How does one count in the matrix? In zeros and ones? As zero and one? In the matrix, what was the sum of the two of us, the Good Man and I? I thought we'd become number one, but we ended up less than zero, a negative number signifying nothing.

6. *Math.* A rectangular arrangement of quantities or symbols. . . .

> **1902** *Encycl. Brit.* XXV. 277/2 A matrix has in many parts of mathematics a signification apart from its evaluation as a determinant.

In the matrix, zeros and ones (numbers and people) add up to a multitude and are less than nothing. Their mathematical value is meaningless, but their significance is such that they can make and destroy worlds. Determine their sum: apart.

7. *attrib.* and *Comb.*, as **matrix-maker, -suffocation.** . . .

> **1890** R. Boldrewood *Miner's Right* (1899) 177/2 Many a quaint fragment, or *matrix-encircled nugget, . . was transferred . . on that auspicious day.
>
> **1598** Sylvester *Du Bartas* ii. i. iii. *Furies* 566 Such are the fruitfull *Matrix-suffocation, The Falling-sickness, and pale Swouning-passion.

3. Albert Camus, *The Fall,* trans. Justin O'Brien (New York: Vintage Books, 1956), p. 14.

More or less, zero and one, I fell in love in the matrix. On that auspicious day we lost our breath; it was taken away. Before we knew it, we couldn't talk anymore. We were transformed as we played our games. We wrote by e-mail and breathless we wrote more and more and more. It was always the same game with different players; we just played it on different nights and often with different names. Fruitfully suffocated, or so it seemed, we sat home alone at our terminal sites and talked to each other in quaint fragments. We didn't know where we were anymore. Did it matter what was said and who was speaking? Did it matter if the Good Man was *really* good—or for that matter, *really* there? It was all so terminally bloodless: that pale Swooning passion. On the other side, inside, I nearly bled to death.

To heal, to cauterize. Theory as apocalypse, conflagration: error burned up. Not catharsis, but cruelty. . . . To find the true fire, Semele asked for the full presence of her divine lover, and received the thunderbolt. Hiroshima mon amour. *Save us from the literal fire. The literal-minded, the idolaters, receive the literal fire. Each man suffers his own fire.*[4]

Each woman suffers her own flow alone. So many women with female trouble. How many women do I know that cannot get pregnant because they "waited too long"? How many women do I know who have asked their friends to accompany them to the clinic or hospital where they are going to have an abortion because their birth control method did not work? How many men went with them? How many women do I know who are lesbian and visit gynecologists who presume that they have sex with men? How many women in this country have several children during their teens and twenties because they are not educated about birth control, or because it simply requires too much money or effort to get it? How many women do I know who suffer from such painful periods that they lie in bed with water bottles on their stomachs for a few days of each month? How many women do I know who have contracted sexually transmitted diseases because they were "on the pill" and their

4. Norman O. Brown, *Love's Body* (New York: Vintage, 1966), pp. 177, 182. I have combined two of Brown's aphorisms, à la Norman O. Brown, alchemist of sampling.

partner did not use a condom? How many women do I know who suffer from back pain because their breasts are too large, and cannot receive a breast reduction operation because it is considered cosmetic? How many women do I know who have had their breasts enlarged? How many women have I seen on talk shows who had breast implants in which everything went awry, fell to waste? How many women do I know who hate their bodies? How many of you can say:

1. I am happy as my body.
2. I love my body.
3. I don't care if s/he loves my body.
4. I do not judge others by their bodies.
5. I like pelvic examinations; I like putting my feet in the cold metal stirrups; I like having a stranger put lubricant on his or her glove and shove their thumb into my rectum and stick their speculum and put cotton swabs in my vagina, and talk casually to me or the attending nurse the whole time.
6. I am not affected by mass-mediated images of bodies that are young, thin, and unchanging, ever adolescent.
7. I would rather have the heavy body of Rosie O' Donnell or Delta Burke than the body of Kate Moss or Julia Roberts.
8. I don't often comment on the weight gained or lost by those I know in daily life, and those I encounter in the virtual American Community.

How did you score in this quiz? Do you want to score?

9. I don't wonder if Tori Spelling had plastic surgery.
10. I don't talk about the size of Dolly Parton's breasts.
11. If I were a man, I would read this the same way as a woman.

Date: Mon., 27 Mar 1995 11:38:32 PST
To: S.Paige.Baty@williams.edu
From: "Ad Infinitum.com"
Subject: uh oh

No joke, unfortunately...

SeXXy Software Presents . . .

NOW YOU CAN HAVE YOUR OWN GIRLFRIEND (tm)

... a sensuous woman living in your computer!

GIRLFRIEND is the first VIRTUAL WOMAN. The result of over 15
years of artificial intelligence research now lives inside your
computer. You can watch her, talk to her, ask her questions, and
best of all have sex with her – THE WAY YOU LIKE TO DO IT. Over
100 actual color photographs allow you to see your girlfriend as
you talk to her, guide her into different rooms, ask her to wear
different outfits, or to slowly disrobe for more intimate
pleasures. GIRLFRIEND can be a sweet young thing you've always
wanted to cuddle with or the tireless sexual dynamo you've
always fantasized about. As a true artificial intelligence program,
your GIRLFRIEND starts with a vocabulary of over 3000 words and
will continually LEARN new words, feelings, and ideas. This
program truly GROWS the more you use it.

GIRLFRIEND requires 7 – 10MB of free space. A VGA monitor is
necessary to see graphics. The more powerful your computer the
faster your GIRLFRIEND will respond to you. GIRLFRIEND comes
with the base software and 2 DIFFERENT GIRLS for you to converse
with: LISA is a sweet brunette who is rated R. SUZY is a hot blonde
who is definitely rated X. Additional girls will be added.

Here is a sample conversation (You would be Dave):
    Lisa: "Hi Dave! It's good to see you again. Do you like my
boots?"
    Dave: "I prefer that black velvet outfit."
    Lisa: "I know. You always ask me to wear it. Shall I put it on?"
    Dave: "Yes, please."
    Lisa: "OK Tiger! I put it on just for you! Do you like my pumps?"
    Dave: "That looks sexy!"
    Lisa: "Thank you! Now what do you want to do today?"

    GIRLFRIEND – base kit plus LISA plus SUZY – regular price: $99

    REGULAR PRICE: $120   SPECIAL INTRODUCTORY PRICE: $69
                    ORDER #SG3

When women go to the doctor sometimes they are not taken very seriously. No one took my complaints of pain and clotting seriously for over ten years. By the time I was diagnosed, I had a severe case of endometriosis. I went on the drug Synarel, which induces temporary menopause. It also causes headaches, excitement, sweating, and all the symptoms of menopause. HOT FLASH: I went through my first simulated menopause at the age of thirty. Synarel has side effects, such as possible loss of bone density. I had to stop after four months because I began to have such painful headaches that I could not get out of bed. I was sent in for an MRI, and my brain scanned: okay. My doctor then told me it was a rare, but possible, side effect of the drug I'd been inhaling through a small white bottle covered with blue writing for four months. I was lucky it was not more serious, he told me. It was just the same old drag. I could try a new drug, or get pregnant. The old drug cost $300 for every two-week cycle. I went from ovarian pain to cranial pain, but the cause for both was the same: the blood just didn't want to leave my body. It wanted to make a web of my insides, filled with all the unreleased blood made to feed children I was not to have. Female trouble is costly. The matrix is not always a holy place.

EACH WOMAN SUFFERS HER OWN FIRE— GET WIRED/STITCHED

Date: Thurs., 09 Mar 1995 12:49:09 EST
To: "Dr. Rocket" <S.Paige.Baty@williams.edu>
cc: A Marxist Angle
From: Milan Ginsbyrge
Subject: Notes

This started as a note to myself
but then I figured I should send it to someone
if you don't have time to read it, don't bother.

I cannot differentiate between self and other. I am trying to use Hegel's notion of the master/slave dialectic to begin a dialogue with myself and others. You are an other, as I am to myself. I sometimes think of Freud's theory of penis-envy as one of deferred self. This is a version of the master/slave dialectic, but it is rooted in the body and psyche of woman. Penis envy defines woman as not man, as wanting to fill the lack of herself as the phallus of man. This is related to fascism, which is ironic when we think of Freud's relation to Nazism. How can we have a revolutionary theory without wrestling with the dialectic? Maybe the dialectic, like the state, will wither away under a new order. In that order we would no longer have other and self; master and slave; woman and man. What would we be left with? I know that there is a difference between woman and man, but I do not want to stake that difference in the penis or lack thereof. If I do this, then woman is only an incomplete man. There has to be another way of doing this.

Could I develop a theory of sameness which would sidestep the dialectic? Do I want to do this? What does this have to do with making up a subject? I want a theory where praxis is rooted right in the theory, where there is no difference between the two. Sometimes I think that the answer lies in Marxism. But then there is this thing called history, and all the history of Marxism in the world shows us how botched an applied theory can be.

It's not strength, but it is power and perhaps then freedom.
Like Love.

Schizoid love, power, and freedom all figure in this narrative. You might think of this as a long e-mail addressed to you, the reader. One of its subjects is endometriosis: female trouble. I do not tell this story to elicit sympathy. I do not want sympathy. I want to be taken seriously, or at least listened to. Sympathy is cheap, and offers no permanent cures. In a healthy society sympathy would not substitute for better means of connection, such as federal and state funding for studies of diseases such as breast cancer, HIV, and endometriosis; a better patient-doctor dialogue, a sense of mutuality in which the members of any discussion are engaged in conversation in such a way as to really care about what the person they are talking to is trying to tell them. This requires listening, and patience. This requires time. This requires community. This requires spaces in which such dialogues can take place among persons in communities over time. This requires a sense of history and place. All of these things did not figure in my medical "record." And all of these things, for the most part, did not figure into the e-mail world I was to enter through a virtual stranger met in the matrix of my computer. Here the costs were hidden, and history was all a secret or a fiction.

```
Date:    Sun, 05 Mar 1995 13:02:00 EST
To:      S.Paige.Baty@williams.edu
From:    The Weather Men
Subject: you're

logged on
and wired
to go and
go and go
start new
This disk is unreadable. Do you want to initialize it or eject it?
Initialize.
Initializing this disk will erase all of its contents. Do it anyway?
Yes.
Initializing.
Creating directory.
Verifying directory.
Done.
```

The disk was initialized, and I went forth after erasing all the previous entries on unreadable desktops. I thought that I was beginning again. I thought that I was moving forward but I was getting caught in the net. Now the writing was going two ways: I wrote my books, and I wrote virtual letters. I was looking for an audience. I was "open" to correspondence. I felt myself to be one continuous opening, now and forever, even unto the end of time. It all came down to zero, or writing zero by degrees, or the story of "O." I am honestly not sure what it was I was doing. I thought I was joining a new community, but now it seems that I was a member of the null set. If you ask me what it means, I'll tell you: nothing. I will tell you nothing. I move between present and past: tense. I am not sure where I lived then. I was not sure who I talked with. I was unsure of many things, but this was my virtual opening.

Open is broken. There is no breakthrough, without breakage.
A struggle with an angel, which leaves us scarred or lame. Every
dream is a struggle: the possible confronting the real, abruptly.[5]

5. Brown, *Love's Body*, pp. 185–186.

One day I cracked the e-mail code and was on line—online—online. Breakthrough. I became open to the world at my terminal site. Breakthrough: I was talking to people everywhere and nowhere. I entered the world of ramified dreams. At the end of my dream I confronted the real, abruptly. I had a struggle which left me scarred, but not lame. I spoke to a perfect stranger: he whispered sweet nothingness in my ear. Immaculate conception: would he speak god into my matrix? Would he cure my female trouble? Would I become whole?

```
Date:     Wed, 05 Apr. 1995 14:59:39 EDT
To:       S.Paige.Baty@williams.edu
From:     rusty Heart
Subject:  btw

you are logged on twice
if you would like to prevent others from "write"-ing unto your
screen
and throwing their cyber-shmutz on top of your medic-alert
words
type mesg n
"mesg n"
if you would like to return to the "open" fields
type mesg y
surprisingly, unix also has a built-in feature called the echo.
the echo repeats everything you type into the computer.
it seems more helpful than most "friends."
to see or hear it in action, type
echo random self-affirmation of value, worth, esteem
that's "echo - - - - - - - -" [return]
it is guaranteed to be

1) faithful
2) loyal
3) obedient
4) diligent
5) self-less
6) empathetic
7) clever
8) enthusiastic
9) heliotropic
10) easily eclipsed
```

I never used that particular built-in feature, because I was looking for an echo in another animate being. Searching for an echo I was open and broken. I later became closed and broken. Now I am open, but not on weekends or holidays or at night. With the passing of time I went offline to that kind of breakthrough: posted a note on my person that read "access denied." I was to become my own "mesg n," or maybe a better way to say it is that I became my own answering machine, screening all callers. Eventually I simply went to an unlisted number. But that comes later in the story. Now we are at the beginning where all is hopeful and good. I went on line with a passion equal to that of the infatuated lover. I was thunderstruck by e-mail. I believed for a time in simile, kinship, parity, and reciprocity. None of it came true, and there was no happily ever after on Valentine's Day.

Imagine that this little book is a valentine. Valentine's Day was always my favorite holiday. I loved exchanging simple pre-made cards, and sometimes home-made letters, with my mates. This is a book about what happens later in life, when Valentine's Day doesn't figure in the same way it did when the writer was an eight-year-old girl who made a white envelope and covered it with a doily and put it on her wooden school desk and received gifts of love from the other girls and boys. Yes, this is about death, longing, and belonging, and other kinds of cutting and pasting. This is about virtual valentines. I sent the lines that got me snagged by the net, the kind that got me hooked on the wire of the fishnet empire we call the World Wide Web. When you're caught in the net, you go on a search for an echo.

Imagine now that this is a book about Gopher's Day. The Gopher is not a Ground Hog because he casts no shadow, and he is no weather bane. He is simply a nickname, a tool for searching. Yahoo! The Gopher cracked me up and left me wide open. I entered the virtual world on a whim at a dot com or some kind of "connect the dots" place of being and seeing. A lot of the data is missing from these artificial files. Fill in the empty places yourself. I cannot completely fill those holes for you. Neither can the Gopher, or the walrus for that matter. I cannot be your artificial memory, although I am sometimes the character Dot Matrix. Print: Save Me. I am a poor relation, a bad imitation. I am, however, also human: being. I am; whoever, a human-being.

```
Date:    Tue., 14 Feb. 1995 01:46:47 EST
To:      S.Paige.Baty@williams.edu
From:    Kaupas
Subject: dr. rocket
```

i am the wether bane
of your existence
whether you like it, whether you don't
call us, whether you like it, whether you don't
spin me left and light and i am
still pointing at your future

    This was one in a series of e-mails from a friend. I now ask, is the above statement true? You tell me: I am writing you. Am I? Who is writing what, or who is writing whom? I am not sure where and when I exactly plugged in. Okay, here's my plug: this is a manifesto, written by a cyborg. I am the ghost in the machine that makes white noise. I have a photogrammatic memory: part keyboard, part story, part neuron, part bytes. Watch out, this memory bites back. Call me a writer or a computer hack. This is a story about looking back, told by a woman part Jack Kerouac. We have a lot of things in common; not the least of which is a Cherokee legacy. Legendary authors made up our books. We were fascinated by junk and American dreams. We lived a lot of the same places, or pretended that we did. Maybe we were just haunted by common ghosts. We couldn't get those voices out of our heads so we did the next best thing: we tried to write ourselves.

```
Date:    Mon., 20 Feb. 1995 18:37:40 EST
To:      S.Paige.Baty@williams.edu
From:    Waiting for God.com
Subject: i think
```

i maybe just figured out what was wrong with me
it's that i got sad that my writing is too dense for anyone but
myself
legible only to me.
how much impacted pain. i don't know. it is hard to release the
tooth.
to pull it out.
i fear i may lose it.
when i was a young child, my parents got to
live in their own apartment for a few months.
there was a large playground with a slide that i liked to use. one
day,

when i got to the bottom of the slide, something fell out of my
mouth.
it was one of my baby teeth. in coming down on the ground i had
simply,
easily, painlessly thrown it loose. no string, no doorknob,
just something that flew out of my own mouth and left a little bit
of
warm salty blood in the hole where it had grown.
i want my writing to be that slide. i want you to help me make
that
slide because the only thing we'll leave behind is broken hearts
and
cracked spines.
well-thumbed pages and empty "manos."

Well-thumbed pages and broken spines as writing is redefined in the electronic community to fracture the self. Writing becomes an experience of active alienation. We lose ourselves in places where writers once remembered themselves. We send strange versions of ourselves out into space, and await the messages that may or may not return. We are searching for a way home, or some kind of direction pointing to something. But so often we users are lost. Finding the way on the Internet is not easy. Finding a *real* community is inconceivable, but maybe it is possible to found a history that is retrievable. E-mail trouble is about the ability or the disabilities of those who log on for companionship. I wish them well. I believe that they will learn much about solitude, and hopefully, in so doing, about themselves. They will become lonesome travelers.

On the back of *Lonesome Traveler* there is a blurb I like a lot. It's not even really a blurb, it's more a description of the author. The text reads:

Jack Kerouac (1922–1969), the father and presiding spirit of the Beat generation, once defined literature as "the tale that's told for no other reason but companionship." His novels, which include the classic On the Road, Dharma Bums, *and* The Subterraneans, *make excellent company.*[6]

6. Jack Kerouac, *Lonesome Traveler* (New York: Grove Weidenfeld, 1988 [orig. pub. 1960]), back cover.

What I like about this is that Kerouac made his own excellent company, while he told "the tale that's told for no other reason but companionship." He is one of my Scheherazades in this narrative.

He has made for me an excellent companion. I read *Lonesome Traveler* on a train running the tracks from San Jose to San Francisco. I knew I was a passenger there. I was taking yet another passage, only this time the terrain was familiar. I looked across the tracks for the house I used to live in when I was a child in Millbrae, California.

I saw no traces from the tracks. I had spent the day at Silicon Studios, where I saw a big life-size Marilyn Monroe cardboard cut-out in the locker room, and I wanted to take my picture next to it. There were posters of movies everywhere: *Pulp Fiction*, *Reservoir Dogs*, *Star Wars*, and *Star Trek*. This was a corporation that simulated movies, and I was visiting my friend Ad Infinitum who is a Web architect. He took me to the "campus," and then we got a sandwich, and he left me at the station with my bags—dropped off like so much emotional baggage at the crossroads. I felt an uncanny affinity with Jack. I was on a train, and it was homeward bound, but it was also the City of New Orleans. It was not night time. The conductor kept talking to me. I got stuck on that train.

CUT/BACKPACK/JACK KEROUAC/SO MUCH MORE TO SAN JOSE

I was using the 50 mile ride from 3rd street as my library, bringing books and papers in a little tattered black bag already 10 years old which I'd originally bought on a pristine morning in Lowell in 1942 . . . and so a bag so bad a brakeman seeing me with it in the San Jose yard coffee shop said whooping loud "A railroad loot bag if I ever saw one!" and I didnt even smile or acknowledge and that was the beginning middle and extent of my social rapport on the railroad with the good old boys who worked it, therefore becoming known as Kerouayyy the Indian with the phony name and every time we went by the Pomo Indians working sectionhand tracks . . . I waved and shortly thereafter I read a book and found out that the Pomo Indian battle cry is Ya Ya Henna, which I thought once of yelling as the engine crashboomed by but what would I be starting but derailments of my own self and engineer.[7]

7. Kerouac, *Lonesome Traveler*, pp. 69–70.

Ya Ya Henna: this is a story about a journey and a battle. This is a story about a lonesome traveler. I was on that train, the train I used to ride with my mother to her job in San Mateo. In those days the train was all passion and paradise. The conductor was kind of sort of in love with my mother. She would take me to the Fuller Paint store where she worked and I would pull samples of wallpaper from the books to decorate the Barbie house I was busy building at home. My mama was busy building whatever kind of house she could for her children after my father was gone AWOL. We were both home-makers, only in those days the homes I made were for dolls, and for my mom it was the house of the seven fables. You can select any fairy tale you like to get you through this evening. I prefer sampling.

It is no wonder that this text is a sampler: I grew up a ragpicker of the ruling elite, ripping pieces out of the books they'd use to wall-paper their rooms and switching strip samples of color for testing the ways they would paint their walls. I used these samples as a litmus test for the future I thought I would build. I learned to cut and paste and sample with the best of them: a shoebox for a car, and a fruit crate for a house. It was Malibu Barbie gone crazy. I had more toys than any kid did on the block. Everyone wanted to play with me. I walked with my mother to the cowfield at the end of my street and stared at the animals at dusk when the telephone wires were buzzing and the stars were coming out and my mom was finished with her day and there were tumbleweeds and snakes and my mom told me scary stories before I went to bed and we never missed church for twelve years straight. This was how we lived, and there were five of us. This was the house that lack built.

The thing was, I kept on building. I made a practice of using whatever tools fell before me: found parts. This is my separate piece, made up of some of those found parts. This is a kind of fallen art, made in the darkness of my heart after I grew up and my mother was not at home every night to hear whatever story I had written that day, or to see me act my part in the many plays I was involved in as a child. I always believed that I could make anything, and from this it followed that I believed that I could be anything. I was the jack of all trades. "Jack in and Jack off," one of my e-mail correspondents—let's call him Neal Sembre—described my relationship to quick word games after one of our e-mail correspondences. Actually, this is how Neal Sembre described me in a list he wrote about all the people who would be attending the reunion in the city of New Orleans. I had asked for facts about this strange event to which I had been virtually invited, and he was giving them to me. He made me up, as a fact. He had never met me at the time, and I did not know him. I was going to go spend a week with him and some of his friends as a matter of course, or a kind of freak accident. The idea of a reunion with a group of strangers would make for a good story. That journey crashed. It is the pre-text to this book. It began with phantom correspondence and ended with despondent Post-it Notes. I had no real idea of what I was in for, but I searched the mail for clues. I thought I could figure things out, and as it turns out I was wrong. The road signs were there all along, now that I look in the rearview mirror. And so when Neal Sembre wrote to Paige Baty @ williams.edu the text following the initial invitation read:

```
Date:     Sat, 18 Feb. 1995 22:31:27 CST
To:       S.Paige.Baty@williams.edu
From:     Neal Sembre
Subject:  Dr. Friedrich S. Wilhelm Paige Rocket
```

Hi. Please note the small bugle on my stamp (it's on the other side). I am reminded of, "We can say it; I don't know what it means, but we can say it?" Why? Must be the temptation of the duel, the sense that pistols at dawn might not be best for me. Were Hemingway's friends nice? Think. Hemingway's friends. Bullfighters. Soldiers. Waiters. Journalists. Gary Cooper. Interesting? Sure. Funny? Yeah. Fond of good times? Uh-huh. Honorable? You bet. But nice? Not fucking likely, is it? But what if they lived in places like Burlington or Portland? Would they have succumbed to the mellowing vibes of those rest areas along the road to fascism? Maybe. But wait, I said I wasn't gonna' duel, and here I am writing bad prose.

Okay, a more direct approach. Will this crowd be nice to you? No idea. Still don't know who's coming, and in these matters the mix (like the body) matters. It's been said that if most of us are nice enough one-on-one, my friends, my brothers and I are hellish in any combination that includes two or more of us. Others have

found us a joy to hang out with. So I can't think of anybody
who found us a joy. (Okay, yeah, there's a cheat in there:
those who found us a joy joined in and are now part of the
hell.) Frankly, expect George to be hostile, the Good Man to be
indifferent, Dr. Hilarius to be viciously sarcastic, and Juliet to
be glad to have somebody who might help her take the rest out
back and kick some ass. I, of course, am the nicest guy in the
world; why else would I have friends like this?

Aside from that I'm also slow. I forget that we're talking about
social matters, about relations not absolutes. I'm sure my friends
won't be nice, but you might get along with them. Problem is
you're an unknown quantity (and quality). So let's rewind a bit.
Tell me Paige, are you nice? Is sarcasm fun for you? What do you
make of flat-out mindless fun? How about cruelty as fun? Not
cruelty to animals, verbal cruelty? Do you like Monty Python,
George Romero, John Waters and jokes about dead babies? Do
you understand the brilliance of Evil Dead II? Have you ever been
kicked in the head with an iron boot? No, of course you haven't:
nobody has. I myself am appalled by all of those sorts of things
and would never indulge in any of them. They just seemed like
good starting points to get the conversation going.

Oh, hell, what's the point. Fact is, we're all old, over the hill, lost
our edge. Just a bunch of nice, old guys who like to get together
and have a little innocent fun without hurting anybody's feelings,
never mind destroying property. Really, we're quite dull when you
get down to it. After all, we are professionals. Thankfully, there
will be all that music and food and drink and so on or we'd be
bored out of our minds. Come to think of it, maybe that's why
we're usually nasty--lack of anything else to do. Now there's
an insight for you; write it down cause it'll be on the test.

Why was Neal Sembre writing me in this way? I was a virtual
stranger to him, and he was getting a fix on me. We had met on the
Internet. The closer it came to our *actual* meeting the more complicated our relationship became, or rather, so became my multiple
relationships with his e-mail circle. I went into that circle for a few
days, and I will tell you about it. I will tell you, but not yet. I thought
the point of *e-mail trouble* was the journey to the city of New Orleans, and maybe it was, but it wasn't about those people. As "The
Good Man," another virtual stranger, said to me after a long and
frustrating phone call, "You are fighting your own demons." I found
out that he was right in the end, or maybe before, but it took me a
couple of months to process the whole thing with my hard-driven

memories. Maybe it's always about fighting your own demons, but it takes going through the fight to figure out that is what you are doing. It is a lot easier to blame things on something or someone else. I cast no blame here on anyone but my past and myself. My host had nothing to do with the viruses I had carried around with me for years. How could he? He didn't know me. He had nothing to do with how I had grown up to be no matter how much I was used to imaginary relations.

Did I mention that my father looked a lot like Jack Kerouac? He was a different kind of dharma bum. He used to live in New Orleans. He also died there. It wasn't the flesh-eating virus that got him or a computer virus that caught him: he had a heart attack. Now I'm writing after the fact. He is a lonesome traveler who won't be writing back.

Maybe I should write to someone who can read me, so here is my response to Neal: you got me wrong. I was just a lonesome traveler, as you maybe, probably, figured out later. I was just another dead author drifting through town. I ate brunch at the "Court of Two Sisters," and the waiter took me over to where Tennessee Williams wrote *A Streetcar Named Desire*. This is that story, too. My dad is Stanley. My mom is both Blanche and Stella. Were there any kids in that story? Maybe instead it's *The Glass Menagerie*. I am that girl stuck at home with her mother and the imaginary animals of the mind but I keep coming home and getting caught there. Maybe that's what journeys are about. Ah, Kerouac. Oh, poor Tennessee. Ah, Paige. OHHH, Jack. AHHH, Humanity. Do I really have to choose between happiness and dignity, Jack?

Happiness and dignity plague this fallen Southerner, and I know I am not the first. Tennessee Williams wrote the South. Tennessee: that's where my oldest sister was born. We are all fallen Southerners. We used to sing the "Alabama Anthem" before we went to bed in California. My mother was homesick for the South. She made it up in words for me just about every night; told me stories of dogwood and water moccasins and my crazy grandfather and my dead grandmother and my aunt whom everybody just called "Sister," who went off to live in Indiana with a man she met at the Woolworth's and my uncle Donald who ran away after my grandmother died and he was only about twelve and he followed the circus and later ended up in Texas and he died there a while ago. I grew up in a circle of relatives I had never met, but heard about every night before I went to bed.

So you see from my upbringing that I was used to living among invisible populations of relations. I knew their names, the food they ate, the things they used to do, like one uncle who would only eat burnt toast and had found a legendary hundred-dollar bill in a rotten banana. I don't know if that part was true, but in the Southern fiction I grew up on it didn't matter: it made for a good story. Keep that in mind. I was raised on a steady diet of virtual realities and imaginary relations, chief of which was with my dad. He was almost always absent, but his presence hung in the air like the stale smoke rising from the cigarettes he smoked day and night. His favorite song was "King of the Road." That was Daddy: no phone, no pool, no pets. He couldn't make permanent connections because he was always off somewhere, a lonesome traveler. He was sometimes in Alaska and sometimes Japan and sometimes New Orleans and sometimes Sweden and one time Puerto Rico. He was gone for two-month to five-year periods. One time when I was four he drove up in a car and we were playing on the lawn and I asked my sister, "Who is that man?" and she said, "He is your father," and I said, "I don't have a father," and she said, "Yes, you do and that's him." I didn't recognize him. He was always, for me, inscrutable. He was another Southern fiction: *Gone with the Wind*.

Date: Sun, 30 Apr. 1995 02:35:32 EDT
To: "Dr. Rocket" <S.Paige.Baty@williams.edu>
From: Post Facto
Subject: Too odd

I'm depressed. not clinically. so i found myself looking through old e-mail. from people I used to be friendly with. people who I hate now. I mean people, a person, whom I used to be close with and now literally don't talk to each other anymore (the whole incident, except for the initial fight is in e-mail). Odd stuff. Maybe when you have a lot of e-mail the same will happen to you? (you can edit your life to, just click and erase someone...)

Post Facto was both right and wrong: you can click and erase, but it's not always that easy. For a long time, I did like Post Facto. I lived my life by avoidance, simply not connecting with someone when it was too painful, or difficult, or even inconvenient. E-mail makes it seem as if this is the case, but the residue of your lost correspondence will haunt you. Mama taught me that trick: "I won't think about it today, I'll think about it tomorrow. Hit delete key. After all, tomorrow is another day." The pain appears to vanish, the words disappear into cyberspace. You have put off the pain for another day.

One day I grew up and it was well after tomorrow and the Southern fictions weren't working for me anymore. I could sing "The Old Rugged Cross," and "Pancho and Lefty," with the best of them, but they were not fixing me. Yes, Jesus loved me but the way it came out left me all mixed up and hungry for more. This is part of e-mail trouble, and it is about God and Woman, not at Yale but somewhere else we'll call the institution of higher learning, or maybe the family. I'm still there, only right this minute I'm sitting at an old wooden desk writing away in someone else's house about my family/life. It's not that easy to do, because I was taught different. I was taught to be in the third-person position, but I found out I didn't like living there. It was killing me, and not even softly. I found out that when I was deleting people, I was killing parts of myself. Happy Valentine's Day.

"Kerouac is a victim, a VIC timm of his own i ma JHI NA Tion."[8]

8. Kerouac, *Lonesome Traveler*, p. 7.

Date: Wed, 15 Feb. 1995 06:34:43 EST
To: S.Paige.Baty@williams.edu
From: The importance of being Earnest Hemingway
Subject: i dont
Return-Path: Hidden Garden

think

i liked my
valentine's very much
but maybe im
just a tough audience
but then again
maybe i just didnt
really have that much fun
at all.
so, go live vicariously elsewhere for today.
i will. i am.
this is overrated

Earnest, you may well be right. But now I am sitting here listening to the sound track from *Immortal Beloved* and am trying hard to believe in love. The whole tragedy was based upon a missed communication, a miscommunication, because Beethoven's "Immortal Beloved" never read the letter he sent. If we are to believe the script, this resulted in his ending up deaf and alone. And yet, the same man wrote the music to accompany "Ode to Joy." I begin each day with that ode. He haunts my dreams and thoughts. The soft touch of his fingers on the keyboard is what I imagine as my fingers run up and down a keyboard of another kind. I am not writing, I am not composing, an ode to joy. But, O, Earnest, I love what Beethoven left behind. Is suffering necessary for the creation of something so beautiful? Does being immortal require that one be misunderstood, accused, maligned, difficult to live with, impossible to understand? Can anyone find an echo? Should one even desire so terrible and empty a response from another human being? Or is the longing for an echo just another Freudian or Nietzschean sickness we've internalized and externalized over the centuries? I do not think that I want to find an echo, but I listen to the resounding tones of Beethoven's *Ninth* with a passion and intensity that is frightening to me.

I am hooked on *Immortal Beloved*. I even bought the CD-ROM, which enables me to listen to the *Ninth Symphony*, play weird games, read the Maestro's biography, and compose a little music of my own on my computer. I next bought a coloring book of composers. I bought scores of sheet music, all in German, from the nineteenth century, with all of his music. The scores are all strangely gendered, being either blue or a pale pink. At nighttime I light a fire and two purple candles and I listen to his music and I write poetry in between the lines of that score, that sheet music. It is the only way I have of communicating with him. He was deaf. Maybe somewhere he will read my writing to him, see the shrines I make to him. Maybe I have read too many romantic novels. Maybe I have seen too many movies. It is my suspicion that this is the case as one evening last week I burnt all the poetry in an act of dedication or immolation. I needed to burn it all up. Who and what were being sacrificed in that fire? Was I still stuck on Semele or simile or just bad movies? I cannot say for certain. I know that I am some kind of victim, signaling through the flames.

I burnt my letters to my dead Immortal Beloved, with the high-drama of a Southern dharma bum who likes to see things go up in smoke. Yet I continue to love the letter found among his possessions at his death, a letter he did not choose to burn. It is reproduced on the CD, and I reproduce this reproduction for you. I know a lot is about death, longing, beauty, and desire but I also know it's about disconnection, distance, history, and enigma. I love this letter.

My angel, my all, my very self. . . . my thoughts go out to you, my Immortal Beloved, now and then joyfully, then sadly, waiting to learn whether or not fate will hear us—I can live only wholly with you or not at all . . . Be calm—love me—today—yesterday— what tearful longings for you—you—you—my life—my all— farewell. Oh continue to love—never misjudge the most faithful heart of your beloved.

ever thine
ever mine
ever ours.

L.[9]

9. See the text with the CD for *Immortal Beloved*, Original Motion Picture Soundtrack, featuring the London Symphony Orchestra; Sir George Solti, conductor and music director; © 1994 Sony Music Entertainment Inc.

I am thunderstruck by ellipses. I am eclipsed by Beethoven. I identify with Beethoven. It is a horrible and wonderful thing to do. What has driven me to this form of love or identification? The music, the maestro, the passion the music awakens in me, a weakness in myself, a love for romantic fictions? "My angel, my all, my very self . . ." are these wonderful or terrible words?

Immortal Beloved, my very self. In *Immortality*, Milan Kundera writes:

In our world, where there are more and more faces, more and more alike, it is difficult for an individual to reinforce the originality of the self and to become convinced of its inimitable uniqueness. There are two methods for cultivating the uniqueness of the self: the method of addition *and the method of* subtraction. . .

Here is that strange paradox to which all people cultivating the self by way of the addition method are subject: they use addition in order to create a unique, inimitable self, yet because they automatically become propagandists for the added attributes, they are actually doing everything in their power to make as many others as possible similar to themselves; as a result, their uniqueness (so painfully gained) quickly begins to disappear.[10]

How can we love ourselves and one another? How shall we identify with people, places, and causes without disappearing, or making them over into shadow-versions of our selves? Is it love or immortality that we seek? Or is it simply recognition? I looked for belonging in a virtual world and found that I had disappeared. Now I am coming back, and I need to name myself to do so. I must always remind you that I do so with caution, oh so much trepidation, and then what I believe to be some kind of grace or courage. Otherwise the project would mean nothing for me, and I have had it once and for all with projections. I will not do this by addition and subtraction: I am working with multiplication tables of content and discontent. I am trying to confront the sphinx of myself. This is no easy project for women, and has not generally been so throughout the

10. Milan Kundera, *Immortality*, trans. Peter Kussi (New York: Grove Weidenfeld, 1991), pp. 100–101.

ages. Look at what happened to Medusa when she had to look in the mirror. I would prefer to avoid such a fate. Instead I follow the daughters of Mnemosyne and try to work with nine muses: Clio, Erato, Euterpe, Melpomene, Polyhymnia, Terpsichore, Thalia, Urania, and Calliope.

An image of these women sits above me as I write. It is from the nineteenth century, and is framed in gold. The writing at the bottom of the picture is in Greek. In this picture the muses are dancing. Their hands are held together in a circle of sisterhood and creation. They all wear different-colored garments. They dance with their mother: Memory. Their expressions vary; but not all of them register joy. Still, on they dance above me as I compose myself in this memoir of simulation, or simulation of memory. These muses are images to me, but I know each of their faces. To me each is unique. They have strong calves and their feet seem to never stop moving. Still, they are mute. I know that I must go on with my project, and must try to remember as well as I can while I dance, sing, write poetry, evoke eros, and confront each muse one at a time. It is not always easy, but it is necessary. Like Joan Didion, I tell myself stories in order to live. I feel a need to name things.

Naming things and making them up. Gertrude Stein and I were both interested in *The Making of Americans*. Miss Stein told me:

Every one has in them their own history inside them, in each one the history comes out of them in the repeating . . .

Sometime they each one will be dead and then one will do no more repeating; there will then have been, there will then be a whole history of each one.[11]

The pleasures of mindless repetition. I let out a great "Yelp," and I set about my task. I wrote my own history; I wrote myself letters. I waited for the time when one would be dead, and there would be no more repeating. Still, I repeat myself. In the end it's strictly academic for me. Hooked on Phonics™ worked for me. Ode to Joy in a minor key.

11. Gertrude Stein, *The Making of Americans* (New York: Something Else Press, 1966 [orig. pub. 1925]), p. 198.

I GOT HOOKED ON PHONICS: I listened to it when I wrote these words, gave my testimony. It was part tape, part text. I played them together and wound up: perplexed. The narrator speaks in monotonous tones: I am grown up, but I'm stuck home alone.

Band, Hand, Land, Sand, End, Bend, End, Lend

Mend, Send, Bond, Fond, Pond, Fund

Gang, Hang, Rang, Bang, Sang, Long, Song, Hung

Lung, Rung, Sung.

That about sums it up, but read on and weep. You can listen to this tape while you sleep. You can pretend you're counting, sheep.

Band/Width, Hand/Writ/ Land/ Of the Lost/ Sand/s of the hourglass/ End/Broken/ Bend/Crossroads/ End/Abruptly/ Lend/ Me your ears

Mend/Broken/ Send/Messages/

Bond/Broken/ Attend/Pond/Walden/ Fund/Mutual

Gang/Bang/ Hang/Nigger/ Rang/Phone/ Sang/Karaoke/ Long/ Longing/

Song/Tape/ Hung/Southern Renegade

Lung/Smoker/ Rung/Hung-up /Sung/Over

   If you're hooked on phonics you can read that again. Remember, when you can say it by yourself you've cracked the code. You'll be on line. You'll get hooked. Let's talk about e-mail. Ntalk me, baby. I'll meet you in the mud, or some chatroom in virtual time. E-mail trouble is lousy rhymes: I've seen the future and it's murder: when they said repent—I wonder what they meant? Love's the only engine of survival. Send me a message. It's over. I'll meet you in the future. I'll meet you as a virtual stranger who will come tap-tap-tapping at your window. Things are going to slide-slide in all directions. We are victims signaling through the flames. Call me the Lost Lenore. I am the poet addicted to scores. Who is that tapping on my door? Quoth dead letters: nevermore.

Date: Mon., 13 Feb. 1995 20:38:46 EST
To: Paige Baty <S.Paige.Baty@williams.edu>
From: Peter Rabbit
Subject: RE(A)D ME(AT)!

Hey here it is...Cultures of Addiction

Addiction has become an obsession in contemporary American
political culture, and figures prominently in the global
imagination: from the rhetoric of talk shows, fetal alcohol
syndrome, eating disorders and the "War on Drugs," to the mass-
mediated identities of cultures such as Columbia, Cuba, and Haiti.
Aside from its contemporary relevance, addiction has been an
integral constituent in the identities of cultures, particularly in
the interaction of the west and eastern/"oriental" countries such
as Thailand and China. We would like to study the problem of
addiction, particularly the ways in which technology informs it,
from a multi-disciplinary, semiological, and cross cultural stand
point through a study of the fiction, history, theory, and science
(particularly in the fields of biology, computer/information, and
Neuroscience) of addiction.

Issues on which we will focus on are:

*   The relationship between AIDS, addiction, and technology. As
     a point of reference we would use the interplay in Thailand of
     heroin addiction, prostitution (sex-addiction), and the rapid
     dissemination of the HIV virus facilitated both inter and intra-
     culturally (Thailand-Japan; Thailand and the "West") by the
     increased "mobility" technology affords.

*   The relationship between advances in fields of technology
     and addiction. We would consider issues such as: uncovering
     Genetic "predispositions" for addictions, current methods of
     treatment for addicts and alcoholics, Insulin "dependence," the
     historical responses of cultures to the "problem" of addiction
     and how advances in such fields as genetic engineering might
     inform these responses.

*   Technologically based forms of addiction such as:
     televangelism, mud usage, vidiots, talk-show junkies, and
     e-mail users.

*   Addiction as a mechanism of power and oppression: the British
     "opening up" of China via opium, Cuba and Tobacco, American
     inter-cities, and sufferers of eating disorders.

*   The malleable figuring of the addict in the "information age"
     from hardwired transgressor to correctable victim, and the
     dichotomy between sanctioned addicts (executives on prozac)
     and outlawed ones (the inner cities on crack).

These are the confessions of an e-mail addict. I am writing after I've kicked, gotten clean, given up on virtual strangers and electronic connections. But addiction has to figure somewhere in this account of love, memory, belonging, and the Internet. I was desperately seeking something or someone and I thought I could find it in virtual time and space. As it turned out, this was not the case. But I had to take a long, dazed journey into myself to find this out. Was it about the addict or addiction? Was it about the project or projection? Was it fact, myth, fantasy, or fiction? Did any of this *happen* at all? What's happening when there is no there there? Somebody else do a phenomenology of that. I'm just trying to tell a story. But who is my audience? Am I searching for someone to call "My Angel, My All, My Other Self"? Am I seeking an immortal beloved, or immortality itself?

I believe that now I can answer honestly, "no," to at least one of those questions, but I cannot say for sure, and I won't tell you which one. This is an honest program. I continue to try and answer them, and these answers matter more to me than the correspondence I was engaged in when I suffered from e-mail trouble. I was Job, or it was about my job, or it was about anomie, or it was about seeing a lot of people I loved crash, burn, or die. I had lost faith, and I set about fervently seeking some substitute for what I thought I had lost. As was the case with Job, most of what I thought I had lost has now returned to me, in greater and unimagined ways. I do not regret the journey, nor do I claim an "arrival." I am simply regaining faith and remembering grace. For awhile I forgot these things, and I paid a price for this. I also gained a great number of things in the process. Sometimes I think I gained an Emersonian version of self-reliance, but then I am immediately reminded of the fact that what matters most to me are those I love. I seek now a balance between self-reliance and love of community. Perhaps I am not so unlike Emerson at all: "Solitude is impracticable, and society fatal. We must keep our head in the one and our hands in the other."[12]

12. Ralph Waldo Emerson, *Society and Solitude* (Boston: Fields, Osgood & Co., 1870), p. 20.

Here is a story about the kind of community and communion I want. It is an ordinary day, and I return home and check the mail. Among the awkward pile of flyers and bills is a gift of grace. I receive a letter in the mail from my friend who is a deaf actress. She has had a nightmare. She cannot call anyone because she cannot use a phone. She does not at this time have e-mail. She writes by hand, and the pages number fifteen. The pages are enclosed in a mass-produced card. The card features a woman standing nude in a tub of water. The word "water" is written upon the drawing of water in the tub. The woman is walking on "water." The caption on the top of the card reads, "Her first steps, though cautious, began immediately to reinforce her faith in greater possibilities." I love this card from my friend, but I love her letter more. My friend Tuesday Grace writes to me:

I decide to try and sleep again so I think of things that make me happy and I thought of you. I miss you. I can't tell you how long the days were when you were gone. I imagined I was going to come to the city and emerge as Miss Intrepid New Yorker—and while I did do some amazing feats of independent organization, I am largely lonely and bored and hungry for friends. Oh sure "Go to the museum," you say, "You live in the culture capital of the world." But I have to reply, "There's only so much I can enjoy doing by myself." Eventually I am overwhelmed with dissatisfaction and a terrible anxiety that no one will know how I felt when I was here. Maybe that is why people write "Rhonda was here" on the bathroom wall.

Grace never ceases to amaze me. I am blessed to know her. I think about her moving around in the world with people thinking she can hear when she can't and I think about how hard she tries to talk and connect with people and I am overwhelmed with a desire to call her, which I cannot do. In this case would e-mail be a form of being with grace? Certainly people who cannot hear gain access to communication by the increasing presence of e-mail and Ntalking. But I do not think that a virtual interaction is what Grace was longing for. Grace wanted the impression of human flesh. Grace wanted to transcend the text. Grace wanted to make her own impression: for people to know that she had been here. I don't think that could have happened on the Internet. This single letter from Grace means more to me than all of my e-mail correspondences combined. I will always keep it. It is written by hand. It was written across time and space and it was addressed to me, by someone who loves me and whom I love. And there is the simple truth of it, and I add this by way of explanation and comparison with what is to come.

Date: Sat., 08 Apr. 1995 13:22:08 EDT
To: S.Paige.Baty@williams.edu
From: The Tin Man
Subject: you seldom

seem to get the mail
i send you, so as a
check, tell me if you
get this. it's just science.

Such was the daze of e-mail and my life in virtual reality. I had acquired a tin man's heart, only to find that the man behind the screen was nothing but a projection. What sad song was going through my head those days: "If I only had a heart." I wished to Oz for a heart, and I received one but it wasn't the one I really wanted. I cast headfirst into the Internet. I got hooked. I bled meaning. I tried breathing, but I was stuck at some terminal dock site so I flailed like a fish out of water. Poor fish, stuck in the Internet. I got stuck. This is a story about the wrong kind of wishing. The first rule is: don't wish for everything. You might end up with the tin man, clicking your shoes together, praying to get back home. You might say, "I surrender: Dorothy." You were not a writer: you were a hacker. You were not an achiever: you were a slacker. You were just one in a sea of faces. You met a stranger on the beach. You killed him. You did not know why you did it. Yeah, you did it but you did it as a twisted romantic fiction. You call yourself melancholic, but that's just a romantic pseudonym for what you really are. I am a dead author, writing dead letters.

TOPICS OF DISCOURSE

I am a Pisces. Jesus told an apostle he would make him a "fisher of men." On the Internet people become fissures of men. Cast your nets upon the waters. Cast your nets upon the daughters. Sacrifice Iphigenia for the "face that launched a thousand ships." This is my s(Tro)r(y?). Am I Cassandra? Am I Iphigenia? Am I Electra? Am I? Why are so many lives versions of the same story? What's in a name?

```
Date:     Sat, 21 Jan 1995 14:20:38 EST
To:       S.Paige.Baty@williams.edu
From:     Jill Sans Jack
Subject:  type in

chfn
to change your handle
to something else
like, uh, oedipa maas or something
also, if you want to check who else is on e-mail when you are
type finger
and write
if you want to write to their screen like
write pbaty and then type whatever you will - with the control
c button to quit the process
```

In those days I changed my handle a lot. I made up multiple versions of myself and cast them upon the Internet. I could be virtually anyone and no one, everywhere and nowhere at once. I was a spontaneous writer, like Jack Kerouac. Only my beat hero was not a computer hack. He was an author, and now he is dead. Mostly I've made Jack up in my head. But all along I knew that man was dead.

AN ACADEMIC EXORCISM

From "What Is an Author?" by Michel Foucault

The second theme is even more familiar: it is the kinship between writing and death. This relationship inverts the age-old conception of Greek narrative or epic, which was designed to guarantee the immortality of a hero. The hero accepted an early death because his life, consecrated and magnified by death, passed into immortality; and the narrative redeemed his acceptance of death. In a different sense, Arabic stories, and The Arabian Nights *in particular, had as their motivation, their theme and pretext, this strategy for defeating death. Storytellers continued their narratives late into the night to forestall death and to delay the inevitable moment when everyone must fall silent. Scheherazade's story is a desperate inversion of murder; it is the effort, throughout all those nights, to exclude death from the circle of existence. This conception of a spoken or written narrative as a protection against death has been transformed by our culture. Writing is now linked to sacrifice and to the sacrifice of life itself; it is a voluntary obliteration of the self that does not require representation in books because it takes place in the everyday existence of the writer. Where a work had the duty of creating immortality, it now attains the right to kill, to become the murderer of its author. . . . If we wish to know the writer in our day, it will be through the singularity of his absence and in his link to death, which has transformed him into a victim of his own writing.*[13]

Hello, reader. You may recognize me by the singularity of my absence: I am a victim of my own writing. There was no plot. This is not a conspiracy theory. This is an act of contrition. This is written in blood, by a vampire. I am interviewing myself. I am reviewing myself. I participate in the "voluntary obliteration of the self" in my everyday existence. Alas, a lack, I lack a day. A Lass who hacks, who gives away versions of herself: hit/play. The tape is on automatic pilot. I just go over the same things again and again. Repetition. Looking for the signposts on the road to salvation I must have missed. But still, but still, you must remember this. I am haunted by the specter of my virtual history, and by the tracks of the places where I really lived. Can I even use a word like "really" anymore? I think so, therefore I am not sure. I am confronting my demons, or listening to my daemon. One of these demons is San Jose.

13. Michel Foucault, "What Is an Author?" in *Language, Counter-Memory, Practice*, ed. Donald F. Bouchard, trans. Donald F. Bouchard and Sherry Simon (Ithaca: Cornell University Press, 1977), pp. 116–117.

San Jose haunted me and Jack. We couldn't get out of the suburban blues. We read the same authors, and discovered spontaneous writing. Jack is my other father, born through the looking glass of a beat generation: we both wrote in burroughs after chasing the white rabbit down the hole, searching for the holy. We were wild cards: we were poker-faced. We were lonesome travelers, victims of our own imaginations. We loved America, or what we thought it was. Me and Jack. We put our hands in the hole and were bitten by a gopher. Errata Stigmata: we were crazy Catholic mystics bleeding and blending or some kind of happy ending. We did it all for kicks. Silly rabbit, tricks are for kids.

Just kidding. I'm a kid. A white kid glove. This is a woman's labor of love. What kind of codes could me and Jack crack? You were a cracker, Jack. What's the prize inside the box? Where can I turn? Can a woman be a dharma bum, or will she just bum herself out? If you meet Kerouac on the road, kill him. Tell another story, lonesome traveler. Is this just kidding? One little girl keeps looking back at me; asks questions with intensity. She says, "Eat me, Drink me." This is my body I ink. This is my blood: I think. It's all about Jesus, and Dylan and fairy tales gone haywire. I'm stuck in the mire. Alice, my friend, I am a post-maiden hobo. I'm not a man, and I didn't work for the railway and I didn't grow up in Lowell, Massachusetts, but I spent a lot of time there once, and I am haunted by the ghosts of your Massachusetts tracks and memories. Playing games for higher stakes than I knew at the time, because I didn't know how much I had to lose. As it turned out, I had much to learn about loss. I have the scars to prove it.

To: S.Paige.Baty@williams.edu
From: Speedy
Subject: i just hecked

checked not hecked, although hexed would be something you're an authority on, yes?
my answering machine, i checked it, and i laughed really hard in the library when you said "hi this is paige im not here right now" and i miss you already.

Hi, this is Paige, I'm not here right now. That about sums it up. I spent a lot of time nowhere. I was making myself a history. I sent an e-mail and called it a book. I was broken from bending, living too long on my knees: one time Alice asked me, "Do you love trees?" We stayed up the whole night scraping this table I found with forks and knives and Jasco fluid trying to get to its American grain. We mutilated that table. Now I write on it. It is my table of contents. Do you remember carving that table? What were we trying to get back to: the tree that it came from, or the final finish?

Date: Mon., 27 Feb. 1995 12:50:13 EST
To: S.Paige.Baty@williams.edu
From: Oedipus Vexed
Subject: I-glasses

i considered myself an optician
my words and deeds the correcting lens
for those who failed to see the truth and beauty
in nature's perfect symmetry
i was an i for the myopic eye-
the rose coloured glass to tint and
compensate for the near sighted
and provide the true blues for Lennons

and Lenins who sadly could never focus
on the melting sand _below_ the horizon
now i see that i am not a king but an emperor
with new clothes and old spectacles-
the vertigo makes me ill as i stare out
over the precipice of infinite knowledge
with my binoculars backwards
making the world seem so small so containable
so compact

i shall overcome this stigmata when my eyes
adjust to the light streaming into the cave
making truth out of shadows and
day out of night

i pledge never again to super-impose my
own image on those who have their own form
my project is to not project or subject
i am la tabula rasa

i am the photographic plate

i am the transparent eyeball

E-mail messages are windows of the soul, just like the eye. Or is it the "I" that is the mirror of the soul? Shall I mix my metaphors? Shall I eat a peach? I have heard virtual strangers singing, each to each. We all wrote; home, alone. We were never together when we tried to talk to each other. We were apart. We were a part of one another. We were apart from one and others. We were our own others. We used the method of addition and turned other people into ourselves. We screened our calls and screeched our drawls. We shopped alone at random malls. Let's go window-shopping.

OTHER WINDOWS OPENING: The couple across the way from my window are fighting again. I hear them fight day and night. I often hear their children crying. Today she is screaming at him. She is say-ing, "Stop blaming other people. I am sick of the way that you blame other people. You are blaming me. When you blame other people, you blame me. One snide comment after another. Stop that shit. I am not being unintelligible, I am sick of your shit. Stop blaming other people." I am not able to hear what he is saying, as only she is screaming. He is watering the garden, again. He turns the hose on full blast and water comes streaming high in the air, over the fence, into our yard. I am on the second story, at the window. The water hits my face. Baptism by fire? I stop writing to try and figure out why they are at it again.

```
Date:     Fri., 03 Mar 1995 04:07:56 EST
To:       "Dr. Rocket" <S.Paige.Baty@williams.edu>
From:     The Thin White Duke
Subject:  Ash
```

The resonance of my feet on asphalt is too silently haunted. I used to be afraid, under the quilts, I used to hear the noises of my parents' fights as ghosts. The wind slapping the willow against my window; the light under the door from the hallway. Now, I've let the dead, the stripped to the bone and eye, be killed.

I am overwhelmed by the Thin White Duke and so go searching for answers. I am a cyborg, so I stop/scan/Internet access guide for the Delphic oracle. Delphi is an e-mail system. We have confronted Delphic oracles throughout Western history, and they have shot out questions and answers. I read a manual that explained e-mail to me, long after I'd been using e-mail. I was taken aback by the words in the manual. I was led through a textual tour of Delphi-e-mail routes, while at the same time the text was telling me what e-mail was. It was all about connection, disconnection, time, death, and the future.

It was mostly always that way with e-mail for me: I got a list of questions with no answers, and they all pointed to the future holocaust. Or should we say, in virtual time, the hollow costs, the dry salvages? I cannot say I know for sure, but the cost at the time was measured in blood, and life, and flesh and reality for me. Still, I received these dead letters and did not know what to do, how to reply. I am now responding to your e-mail. I am sorry, Virtual Stranger, it took me awhile to digest the soap, the skin, the ashes, the anger, and the anomie. I am not the enemy, just another victim of our century. Perhaps one day you'll *talk* to me. I am not just Dr. Rocket, I am Paige Baty. Keep the difference in mind, gentle, virtual reader. Many are the ways of genocide in our time, many are the ways of terrorism, many are the ways of misjudgment. To err is human, to forgive divine. Deleting people is about killing time. But there is a great danger in killing: you risk losing your self in the process.

Killing time is what e-mail is all about. People kill time as they make themselves up into virtual beings, give themselves new handles as ways of staving off life, or the world at the door, or the wolf at the door. E-mail was about user names. Lots of people use their birth name as their user name, but others create pseudonyms to engage in virtual correspondence. The guide helped explain the system to users. To learn to create an e-mail message, users were instructed to mail themselves a message. The authors tell us, "It doesn't have to be long or meaningful." When the message has been received:

14. Steve Lambert and Walt Howe, *Internet Basics: Your Online Access to the Global Electronic Superhighway* (New York: Random House, 1993), p. 61.

Since this particular message doesn't have far to go, you should almost immediately hear a tone and see a message flash on your screen that new mail has arrived. You probably have a pretty good idea who this message is from and what it says, but let's treat it like a real message and see what can be done with it.[14]

The uncanniness of corresponding with yourself: "you probably have a pretty good idea who this message is from and what it says . . ." What if you don't? Do you have a pretty good idea of who you are and what you mean, even when you're just prompting yourself for answers? Do you respond to the message you sent yourself? Did you lose yourself after you faced the oracle? Did you know who your parents were? Did you wake up one day to find out all those riddles you thought you'd solved were resolved in an ending where you had killed your father and slept with your mother and were both parent and sibling to your children? Do we need some gatekeepers? The sphinx was a gatekeeper and look what happened to her. Do we need a confrontation here? What walks on four legs, then two, then three? Do you see yourself in the answer? Who do you correspond with? Have you cracked the e-mail code or have you cracked yourself? As a cracker of codes I wrote as "Rosetta Stone." Here is a message that Rosetta received in response to a message that she sent. It came from the constellation of bodies we are calling "The Good Man."

Date: Mon., 20 Feb. 1995 14:20:13 CST
To: S.Paige.Baty@williams.edu
From: "Net Worth
Subject: As Per Your Request

sand...glass...silicon...semi-conductor. Am I safe in assuming you
already know that _On The Line_ became "Rhizome" a.k.a. ch.1 of
Thousand Plateaus? "We are tired of trees. Pave them all over.
Why doesn't the government do something? Doesn't the average
taxpayer's view matter anymore?" Did the originally mangled
missive show up in complete form? Rosetta Stone: the keystone
to the tower of babel; the secret of the return; the conductor with
no semi about it. Turn on writing and you turn off presence and
you open a space for saying without looking into the other's eyes
and you plug your desiring machines into the expressing machine
and you transmit a line of flight and then later you fear machines
(Freud's move against Hobbes--no aversions, only desires) that
represence the absent even they never met each other and you
see the da(n/g)gers in their eyes and you want to run across
the lines to erase what was written, to unconduct the semi-
transmitted (to untransmit the semi-conducted, take your choice)
to unplug and recontain your desiring machines and the words
have already escaped and so you ask for _something_ back. And
you get tortured by the other's cruel self-indulgence as they
babble on and on and...and I liked your letter even if (or maybe

because) it was as they say "open and personal." Okay? But I believe in bonding through pain, and I think that our lives and friendships would be much less if we only shared or had good times. Okay, so I'm a Hegelian (however much I try to escape the spirit of gravity): I want (my) suffering to have meaning even if it's only in letting us feel love(d). There it is. And so you see that you are not the only one whose tendencies toward verbosity can be indulged by the fluidity of net-writing. Turn on writing and you turn off presence and you open a space for saying without looking into the other's yawning mouth.

P.S. Get a band aid. "Pray to the god for help. Hold the bloodied glass in front of you. Hold it out toward the god. If you are pure he will add his life to your own, for both are red and holy. He uses his powers upon your blood. He turns your blood clear showing you his words through your blood. Read, believe and know. Now, and only now, wipe the glass on your robe. The message is kept from the eyes of your enemies." Trick from an ancient manual by a helio-worshipping spy.

E-mail pseudonyms and virtual strangers: they all appear to me in the bloodied matrix as versions of the same person. Too much blending in is too much bleeding, unless you're going for a Rothko finish. This still life is not about that kind of writing, or representation. This is imagined more in the figures of Munch. Think of this text as the lyrics to accompany *The Scream*. It is an instrumental piece. Torture, and horror, and vampires, and demons, and bleeding women inform its making. But it is also about women and men and the postmodern. We are all caught up in an Internet of escape-hatch mutuality. To get out press Control: X/C. You can quit at any time. If you don't like the music, hit the delete key.

The Scream, not the dream, of a common language. Let's go on a virtual tour of the world. Let's simulate love and war. Welcome to my museum of horrors, where I wax poetic or rhapsodic at the sight of a mute, earless figure stuck on some bridge to nowhere. This is the abridged version of the text. These are my dispatches off the cuff, linking together high and low and other stuff. This is a raw story, a war story, or a war of the words. War and dispatches and representation and death and love are all about the same bloody subject. It is a western subject, told in eastern ways. The bad dreams all came true. All of Scheherazade's stories could not keep the inevitable silence from settling down upon us. Things are pretty quiet round here now.

Date: Sun, 12 Feb. 1995 23:24:13 EST
To: "Dr. Rocket" <S.Paige.Baty@williams.edu>
From: Jean Claude Van Damn
Subject: Re: second try on e-mail

**Tried to send you a more comprehensive message and fucked up.
I don't feel like writing it over again--the gist of it was that I'm
heading home in hopes that I can be more productive there.**

Happy researching

Re: Searching? I snuck in through the gates of the academy. I am
still not sure how I got here, but the getting was good. I am an
electronic version of a Mary prankster. When I was eighteen years
old I took a three-week bus ride with Ken Kesey's X-Driver: That is
another story called "Bus Stop." Sometime I will tell it to you. It's all
about a whore who hopes some good cowboy junkie will save her.
She meets a guy who used to be a prostitute and is moving west to
do airbrush tee shirts. It is a good story. It is not this story. This is a
love story about e-mail: love means never having to say you're there.
And now for me it means saying "I'm sorry" to all the people I was
never there for. I was somewhere else. I'm trying to figure out where
that was. Bad wishing. When I was eleven I was the lead in that play
about the fisherman and his wife. She wishes and wishes for more
and more. In the end she wants to be god: she ends up a fishwife.
There are bad ways of wishing, and worse ways of loving. Be careful
what you wish for: you might get what you think you want.

*I was sitting in the summer twilight with my friend wishing on
fireflies. He gave me this advice: do not wish of a firefly what it
cannot give you. Wish on what is in the nature of the firefly: a
meeting with a friend, a good dinner, a morning walk, a good sleep.
Do not wish for success; or love dying eternal, or capital, or a degree in something or the other. Wish for simple things.*

Grown-up women wish for all kinds of things; not the least of
which is at times a good man. I wished, at a certain moment in my
life, for this. He would take care of me. He would be kind, and good,
and gentle. He would bring me eggs and English muffins in the
morning. He would not be threatened by me. He would have his
own sense of vocation. He would have a sense of humor. For him,
life would be a constant adventure. Maybe he would fly planes for

fun. He would be a real feminist. He would give me space. He would be a kind and generous lover. He would forgive me my shortcomings. He would always be on hand to lend a kind ear. He would always be there for me. PRESS: SAVE.

I wished and I wished and I wasted my days. I thought that I was in love with someone: the perfect correspondent. Let's call him Racer X: Speed's long-lost brother. Racer X. He was a daring character, the crossed-out sign; racing and erasing. A lot of my relationship with Racer X was about erasure and death. We were never in the same place for very long: we met at the tracks. He had a quick wit. He was a computer whiz. He was my long-lost brother. I met him in *real* life. I have known him for many years. He became an e-mail correspondent, too, but mostly X and I spoke on the phone. We spoke on the phone because we were never in the same place. I became dependent on those X phone calls: I felt I had found kinship, parity, community. X marked this spot. Autobiographies and signatures. X.

```
From:    Speed's Long Lost Brother
Date:    Thurs., 30 Mar 1995 12:40:25 -0800
To:      Dr. Rocket
Subject: uh oh
```

How about honesty? Where do you stand? Take a stand there.
of course you are still my friend. to the bitter end
but you are not fully honest with yourself
ad-mit you are torn and need time
and i will give it to you
let's stop playing games
and start learning to trust one another
paige.

I would like to be able to say:

"Hey, Paige, fall in love with someone and still remain my friend. You can have love. We can do great things together." However, you have a really poor track record with romance (although a good one as a friend).

"Why not find someone like....Abraham....oh oops."
"Why not find someone like....Bartleby...oh right [smacks forehead]"

Even the less damaging of the relationships like Soren or Friedrich were bad.

Why do you have bad romantic relationships?
Why do you always have to look at them as Queen/King pairings?
Why do I sound like a Dianetics ad?
In the case of Soren he could never be the King to your Queen,
so you lacked respect for him as a person.
That is a really bad way to look at the person you are in love with.

I understand that you are lonely and afraid that you might not
have the romantic love that you want, but I think that you are
imperiling our friendship and hurting yourself. Relax. Lots of
people love you.

You possess grace in your life, possibly in larger amounts than
anyone I know.

--end of correspondence--

Was it correspondence? I thought so, but at the same time I questioned this form of corresponding. I questioned his questions. It was a series of ridiculous questions, again and again. I thought I was in love. Maybe I thought it was love because it was mostly a one-way relationship. I was told by the fisherman repeatedly that he loved me "as a friend." I wanted love that would transcend. I wanted love that would never end. He saw it differently: he thought that what I wanted was to consume him in a thunderbolt. He accused me of all kinds of things. He thought that I wanted to make him into my audience. He said that I was like Henry Adams, collecting a c/lover that would die. He said that I was not to be trusted. I knew that already. As it was, I doubted my own instincts. I was looking for someone else to take away my doubts, to fill up the hole of myself. I thought that in his gaze if we could see each other I could become real. He would make me happy. He would put me at ease. I craved those moments. He was an Irish ballad sung by the Furies. I was pursued by the furies. Can women have an Orestes complex and an Electra complex at the same time? It sure seemed like it. Oedipus Rex and Racer X met at a series of junctures. Sometimes they worked as a team. Sometimes they fought as mates. The fisherman and Racer X were the same person. Oedipus put out his eyes to save his ego.

```
Date:          Thurs., 30 Mar 1995 11:51:25 PST
To:            "Dr. Rocket"
From:          Racer X
Subject:       Re: uh oh
In-Reply-To:   "Dr. Rocket"
"Re:           uh oh" (Mar 30, 2:21pm)
```

On Mar 30, 2:21pm, Dr. Rocket wrote:
> Subject: Re: uh oh
> I will not go gently into that dark night.

Rage, rage, against the dying of light!
How apropos, since you have been nicknamed Rage.
"She's literally all the Rage!"

> My birth never stops happening every day I am more alive the
> pictures of me for Veiled Threats are beautiful. I glued jewels all
> over my face. The hot glue hurt but it stuck like blood. We did
> the shoot. She shot me at the cemetery. for the shoot the light
> was beautiful I stood for a time in a timeless mausoleum jesus
> window blue behind me framing me I was shot with light shot
> through with the christ i bleed blood like Jesus

Have any premonitions concerning the LAPD?
Will Leslie play Al Cowlings, loyal until the end?

Consumer Reports says that the Bronco is *the* most unreliable
used car to buy. That's why I am not getting one.

You've transcended humility, how about transcending self-pity?

--Oedipus Rex

Why do I share this correspondence, or lack thereof with you? I
am trying. I am trying to be honest. I tried to know Oedipus. I was a
sphinx who could not overcome his Jocasta and dead father. I am
glad that I did not become his Antigone. All the relations were too
much for me. The fallen ways of his family could not be soothed by
any of my Ivy League attempts at speech. At a certain point I stopped
trying. I want to share this with you. Some battles are worth walking
away from. You do not need to fight every dragon. You do not need
to be a Princess. You need to remember where you came from, and
you need to be able to let go. This is a story about letting go, but
first I had to learn about what it was to hold on to the edge of the
abyss, and look down. You, too, may need to learn this.

CUT/PASTE/LOVE'S BODY

Separation (on the outside) is repression (on the inside). The boundary between the self and the external world is the model for the boundary between the ego and the id. The essence of repression, says Freud, is to treat an inner stimulus as if it were an outer one; casting it out (projection). The external world and inner id are both foreign territory—the same foreign territory.[15]

The pseudonym is the externalized id. It is an I.D. made up of projection. It is the naming of the foreign territory between the external world and the inner id: the same foreign territory. Who gave you your name? Did you rename yourself? How often do you use pseudonyms? Are all names somehow "pseudo?" *Shall I project a world?* Where shall I make an address of this "I"? Why does everything bleed into one-ness or nothingness for me? What is for me? What is forming "me?" *The Content of the Form* is a book written by Hayden White. Once he told me he liked that title because no one ever gets it right. This makes sense to me. We spend a lot of our lives confusing content and form. There is no difference between content and form; form and content make all the difference. It was a lack of content that got to me. I was not content. It was a lack of form that destroyed me: I did not remember where I had come from. I was absent. This is my meta-history, because that's the only kind of history I could have at that time, or maybe, all the time. What's your theory of your sign? This is a table of contents of the form.

THE AUTHOR IS QUERIED ABOUT HER I.D.

Date: Tues., 11 Apr. 1995 20:49:19 EDT
To: S.Paige.Baty@williams.edu
From: The Good Man
Subject: Re: My favorite, myself

Dear Paige:

You never did answer why you go by the name Dr. Rocket. Or am I just missing the obvious?

15. Brown, *Love's Body*, p. 148.

> Lucretia says you look like
> the young Bob Dylan, or did when you were younger.

I did. Unfortunately, I'm older now so I don't look like the young Bob anymore. Fortunately, I don't look like the old Bob (just haven't developed the jowls). I look a lot like myself, only backwards.

> so i don't think either of us is crazy at all that's what
> I think.

I'll take your word for it. I had a lot of fun (although you said you enjoyed that reading of Eliot, and so did I, but that was actually during our much shorter phone conversation on Sunday. Which, of course, goes to prove absolutely nothing, except that maybe sleeping better than you gives me a slight edge in distinguishing one day from the next.)

> Today I listened to Dylan and thought about meeting you and
> was happy and apprehensive at the same time.

Don't be too apprehensive. I am a nice person (at least I think so). I am looking forward to meeting you, and hope that you are as happy to meet me when you actually meet me as you are in expectation of doing so. Or whatever. You know what I mean? What if, after all this buildup, I turn out to be completely opposite of your expectations? Maybe I'm just a convenient screen for certain projections you've got going. I'd hate to disappoint you because I'm who I am and not who you're thinking of. But I am who I am and actually like me quite a bit, so maybe you will too once you meet me and sort me out from who you may be thinking I am.

I had a dream about you the other night. You had short hair that was dark brown at the roots and dyed gold or blonde on top. Your eyes looked very familiar, though. I wonder if this dream image looks at all like you (I know the hair is wrong, but the rest, who knows?)? I am mildly psychic, but not in a linear kind of way. My officemate Barbara walked into the office the next day and she had a new haircut and I was disoriented for a second because I didn't recognize her and she sort of looked like the you in my dream, but she has short dark hair and dark eyes and high cheekbones and fair skin (which is how you described your current self) and for some reason I flashed on thinking that it was you. Really weird. She commented on how strange I looked at her. My life seems to be full of these small things like this lately. I like it, but it feels strange sometimes.

Maybe you're not crazy. Myself I'm never quite sure about.

Which Dylan album were you listening to?

What's your favorite color?

And why don't you like beards?

The Good Man *end of query*

DISPATCHES

Talk about impersonating an identity, about locking into a role, about irony: I went to cover the war and the war covered me; an old story, unless of course you've never heard it. I went there behind the crude but serious belief that you had to be able to look at anything, serious because I acted on it and went, crude because I didn't know, it took the war to teach it, that you were as responsible for everything you saw as you were for everything you did. The problem was that you didn't always know what you were seeing until later, maybe years later, that a lot of it never made it in at all, it just stayed stored there in your eyes. Time and information, rock and roll, life itself, the information isn't frozen, you are.[16]

The theorist and the war correspondent do the same work. They think that they can know a little bit about you for their files, and in the end they face themselves, if they are real correspondents. They find out that they are "responsible for everything they saw" as much as for "everything they did." If they have courage, they learn to live with the consequences of what they did. Or sometimes they become Hemingway and shoot themselves in the head. They cannot live with what they saw and did. They cannot find a clean, well-lighted place. They go searching for themselves around the globe. They try everything, but it doesn't work for them. At the end, they feel dried up and dead. They are victims of their writing.

Repetition: I was fighting my own demons; I was writing myself.

I searched for answers posed by Socrates' Daemon. Was I truly no wiser than anyone else? Why was I a woman? When I was eight, the world was my oyster and I was the walrus, or was I the carpenter? I grew up to look for pearls of wisdom in the sands of my youth.

16. Michael Herr, *Dispatches* (New York: Avon, 1978), p. 20.

I always loved sifting through things: like sands of the hourglass, those were the days of my life. *Wind, Sand, and Stars.* I lived on automatic pilot: I did not need a match to light my flame. I burned and I burned and I yearned and I yearned. I was Joan of the fallen arches: Joan of the dark night. I fought windmills and mills and everything that stood in my way. I was a super hero: I was Batman, Superman, the Green Lantern, The Silver Surfer WHAAAAm. Bam. Thank you, man. Pow. Kazow. Right kick to the neck. Hard punch in the chest.

When I was eight, I fought in ways that I do not now understand. Now, everyway I look at it I lose. I was a heroine, not a super hero. I stopped believing in super heroes. I searched and searched and was more and more bewitched, bothered, and bewildered. Where was I? Oh yes, I found myself when I was signifying: nothing. Everything was less than zero. Too bad that I suffered from that complex: do you feel like zero when you're not number one? I felt like "O." O my god.

I know that this work is autobiographical. It comes from my perspective. I suffer from graphomania. I tell stories all night to keep out the inevitable ending. On the other hand, what I'm talking about is all over anyway. This is the story of a thousand and one nights. There are stranger fictions, and I know them, or I used to. Many of my correspondents became stranger fictions. They were no longer real. Truth is stranger than fiction. Truth is a stranger to fiction. Fiction is stranger truth. This is the only way I could tell this story, so this is how I told it. What else should I be—all apologies?

SOMEONE TRIES TO INTERVENE

```
Date:    Wed, 08 Feb. 1995 10:06:27 EST
To:      S.Paige.Baty@williams.edu
From:    Speedy Subject: still

feeling guilty, I am, that is
i don't know what i'm supposed to do
but i guess what i think i'm supposed to do is just not right
because i don't write, either way, to you or for credit
maybe i'm just a negligent student and then a bad friend
```

in that order, a short-order chef.
SO, fry me up some more guilt, I can hash it
together, and maybe it won't be so bad if I catch up
if, when, ever
you maybe don't see how i care
so maybe i don't care as you can see:
ostensible is somehow defensible
but not from my perspective tv
don't change the channel
i'm just on a commercial break

STEP FOUR: *Make a searching moral inventory of yourself.*

And now a word from the author: all right, already. Maybe this is my apology; however, I am; and never was, Socrates. I don't apologize like him. He is another dead author. He never wrote anything. Plato made him up for us. He died for his philosophy. He died for immortality. He died for his principles. He drank a glass of hemlock, out of a sense of duty and obligation. He died for a city-state nation. His mother and father were the laws. Mother and Father in-laws. This story involves tragedy, it involves death, it involves disconnection: it took place in virtual time. It was written in California. I wrote it by myself. Maybe it is really a postmodern slave narrative: *Incidents in the Life of Anna Graham*, written by herself. Slaves had to use pseudonyms to write their life stories, and it had nothing to do with e-mail. They were in hiding from their masters. They changed all the names to protect the innocent. They were fighting *the letter of the law: Webster's definition of the slave as chattel*. They were writing themselves human. These were fugitive acts. They were using the master's tools to dismantle his house. A lot of what takes place in the master's house is horrifying. People are raped, maimed, beaten, underfed, killed, scarred, or left lame.

I know that this is not slave narrative, unless I was a slave to my own imagination. Believe me, there is a huge difference. This cannot be called a slave narrative, but should we try to name it at all? Maybe this is more a computer geek tragedy than a fairy tale. Maybe it is both at once. Maybe it's a French farce. Maybe it's a bad sitcom: Infinity's Company. Imagine me, or some actress, who lives with invisible roommates that appear on the screen as texts. It is an Internet version of MTV's *Real World*, only it is a virtual world. You watch this show, you watch it again and again; and nothing ever happens, like in heaven. A lot of letters are posted, a lot of passion is cast in the role of a woman who looks backwards and finds herself a pillar of chalk. Pillow talk and slateboard chalk: the people in the virtual world engage in some fractured fairy tale of love, connection, disconnection, and death.

The lead actress is called, for the time, Electra. She is a complex figure. Her father is dead. Her brother is missing. She feels separated from her sister; and she has a complicated relationship with her mother. She spends her days mourning, and longing for her brother to return. She is filled with tears and rage: she makes burial offerings for her father. She re-names herself "The X-Ray Queen." She lives in a small black box with a screen that reflects back to you her image. She is stuck on one image. In this image she is five years old. It is Halloween. She is dressed as a princess. She sits on a wooden floor, with a gold cardboard crown on her blonde head. She surveys the treasures she has collected that night: hundreds of wrapped candies spill from an orange and black bag that reads "Trick or Treat." In the back of the image sits a man. It is hard to see his face. He is dressed in black. He watches his daughter survey her spoils. He sits in a casual pose, with an arm draped over a chair and one leg crossed over the other. This is what was in the black box where Electra lived— where she made herself into a spectacle. She made a spectacle of herself and an altar of her father. Was her father the king, god, or just some man? Why was she a princess? Was it trick or treat?

Imagine that. A princess in a black box. Who is the man in black? Why does he survey her? She looks down. She looks down at the goods. She is only five years old. She does not know that she will grow old. Later, she finds out. But this is an early moment in the sitcom, and so let us warm ourselves with this image as we gather ourselves around an electronic hearth. We were young, once. The world was full of possibilities. We couldn't dream of oblivion, then. We didn't know about oblivion, because it was easy to go to sleep. We'd been out all day playing with toys you later found on the walls of a bar in Brooklyn, FLY-BI-NIGHTLY. We would go to that bar and you would say, "There is my old Leggo set; there is my old Fisher-Price Playmate House." They served us vodka in Dixie riddle cups, with tonic on the side. They gave each of us a set of sticks and a coffee can. We all beat out strangled melodies while a man tried to play guitar. We were lost in that moment, but in a good way. Now that moment is lost: oblivion.

We were two girls who liked to play. We were two girls who liked to smash things up. We were, too, girls once. What happened to us? Is this what it means to grow up? I remember you when you were Fly-bi-Nightly, and everything was compact about you except your car. We drove that car too fast, too far. Did I mention that she was my best friend? Did I mention that she loved me unconditionally? Did I mention that in the end I failed her and she checked out?

Date: Mon., 10 Apr. 1995 21:01:03 EDT
To: S.Paige.Baty@williams.edu
From: The Good Man
Subject: Re: My favorite, myself

Dear Dr. Rocket:

(what does that mean, anyway?)

"I've got friends in low places." Quoth paige:
> From the edges of my death bed and the throes of agony,

Didn't get your last week's e-mail until today, which asked me to call and cheer you up but we did get to talk and even though you were throe-ing in agony you charmed me anyway for four hours.

As for our companions, all I can say is I don't know what Romeo likes. I don't know what Juliet likes. Oh wait, Romeo likes Juliet and Juliet likes Romeo. They really do. A lot. I got to hang out with them when they were first getting to know each other and there was lots of holding hands and staring deeply eye-to-eye and basic sweet oblivion towards everyone and everything around. It was very charming to watch, if you go for that hopeless romantic type of thing (and I do, when I'm not being cynical). Methinks that either (1) you are insane, (2) i am insane, or (3) I forget.

> From the west down to the east,

The Good Man <

Romeo and Juliet do not signify the only kind of love. There are many ways of loving, some better and some worse. Some kinds of loves are about twinning. Miss O'Blivion and I were kinds of twins. We were, for a time, kin. If she had a complex, I'd call it the Antigone complex. She was, for a time, a beacon of light. She fought her battles with courage and honesty. She fought and fought and fought and felt defeated. The last time I talked to Antigone I called her to tell her that my father was dead. "Why should I care?" she said. "You always said that when he died it wouldn't touch you." Antigone, I was wrong. You went into a cave, which is another name for matrix.

But the story is not over yet and one day I hope to hear that you didn't hang yourself in that cave, that you girded up your loins and went out again to do battle with Goliath and yourself. We are together in my dreams, but we don't talk anymore. Do you want to talk to someone? Maybe Electra and Antigone could join forces like Maggie and Hopey and be comic book heroines. That's the kind of heroines we should be. There are many kinds of heroines. Mostly they end up young and dead, like Ophelia or Antigone or Juliet or Cassandra or Hedda Gabler or Marilyn Monroe. I hope that we can be other kinds of heroines, and that we end up on altars, not in boxes.

Remember making our altars? At one time the box was not black; it was gold. You covered it with plastic jewelry and pictures of space ships and old subway tickets and Mardi Gras beads. You gave it to me to keep my things in. I looked down, then, and didn't see all the good you gave me. I am sorry. I wish I'd been a better person; but I couldn't have been a different person. I just could have acted different. I'm getting better, and I'm acting less. This is the pre-cursor to e-mail trouble, and I am writing you after history. We could have been young girls forever; but instead we grew old and got ready to die. Part of this was leaving each other and going out with men. Men. Ah, men. We should have written other fairy tales than the ones we did. You could have been Alice, and I should have been Gertrude. Now I see through the looking glass darkly, but one day we may meet face to face.

DEAD LETTERS CONTINUE

Date: Thurs., 23 Mar 1995 16:29:11 CST
To: S.Paige.Baty@williams.edu (Dr. Rocket)
From: Frank Lee
Subject: Re: Hi

> I just got back from these meetings and then San Francisco. It
> was one of the most difficult things of all times because about
> one half hour after that sorry. I will write in a minute, because
> I keep getting interrupted. Paige.

Paige,
This is a wonderful note. Never before has an event in my life so
closely resembled those mystical moments in thrillers when the
main character hears from a damsel in distress or key witness
who is then suddenly dragged away from the phone by
unidentified forces.
If only I were close enough I could rush over to look for clues.
Assuming you foil your attackers, I look forward to hearing how
you are, and about your travails (and travels).

Frankly, he had absolutely no idea about the status of my life at
that time, but I can't say I blame him. He didn't know me. What was
he to do? We were involved in a big narrative game and we were
just two of the players. This is a dispatch from one of the players. I
welcome all others to write or right their own version of the text.
This text is a bridge. This text was written from ground zero. (Have
I mentioned "O" was a kind of Oedipus Rex, or maybe more than
Oedipa Mass? She was always searching for something, call it what
you will. Pynchon called it "trystero." First O called it God, then O
used to call it longing. Now O thinks more like Michael Ignatieff,
and calls it "a language of belonging."[17]

In *American Monroe* S. Paige Baty wrote about the language of
belonging:

*In the face of simulated political culture, a political theoretical
discourse indifferent to attachment, location, and human obligation and relation soon becomes a dead language. Even as simulated discourses become normative, there remains the need for a
civic speech that is capable of mediating between the citizens and
issues of a community of memory, or of simply talking about the*

17. Michael Ignatieff,
The Needs of Strangers
(New York: Viking,
Penguin, 1984), p. 140.

world in which it exists. In The Needs of Strangers, *Michael Ignatieff speaks of the possibility of a civic discourse that attends to human needs in a postmodern society: "Our task is to find a language for our need for belonging which is not just a way of expressing nostalgia, fear, and estrangement from modernity. Our political images of civic belonging remain haunted by the classical* polis, *by Athens, Rome, and Florence. Is there a language of belonging adequate to Los Angeles?"*[18]

The scholar S. Paige Baty was always trying to answer Ignatieff's question. She answered mostly with questions of her own, marked by her disconnection. Her own needs were those of *The Stranger*. Have I mentioned Paige Baty's obsession with Albert Camus? They had a lot in common, not the least of which was a keen interest in suicide. The student Paige Baty read *The Myth of Sisyphus* again and again, staying alive. She wrote versions of it as books, letters to the dead author Camus. She believed, along with her dead correspondent, that suicide was the question facing the philosopher, or, really, all the living. She rolled her books up the hill, but the meaning kept avalanching down again and again. She was caught up in the utilitarian task of making herself over and over again.

```
Date:    Tues., 07 Feb. 1995 12:28:56 EST
To:      S.Paige.Baty@williams.edu
From:    Logged on
Subject: i call you

@ home
but your not
not there
are you elsewhere
or really just not
there - not "at home" so you dont pick up the phone
when i try to call you about radio license and hospital bills
i want to be there to buy the groceries
```

18. S. Paige Baty, *American Monroe: The Making of a Body Politic* (Berkeley: University of California Press, 1995), pp. 51–52.

What was S. Paige Baty doing? She often wondered, and it troubled her greatly. Was she another dead author? Dead authors participate in killing those they know. At the time I was disconnected from my most important connection, and I was looking for anyone to help me find my way back home to myself. I felt that I had lost my audience. I wanted to find that audience again. As it turned out, I looked in all the wrong places.

REPETITION BY KIERKEGAARD AS CONSTANTIN CONSTANTIUS

Although I forsook the world long ago and renounced all theoriz-
ing, I nevertheless cannot deny that because of my interest in the
young man he set me off my pendulum beat somewhat. . . . He
is suffering from a misplaced melancholy high-mindedness that
belongs nowhere except in a poet's brain. He is waiting for a
thunderstorm that is supposed to make him into a husband, a
nervous breakdown perhaps. . . . It is impossible to get involved
with him, and thus it is fortunate that he does not wish for a
reply, because to correspond with a man who holds a trump card
such as a thunderstorm in his hand would be ludicrous.[19]

LUDICROUS LETTERS ILLUMINATE THE TEXT

Date: Wed, 15 Feb. 1995 21:41:45 EST
To: "Dr. Rocket" <S.Paige.Baty@williams.edu>
From: Daniel Webster
Subject: Re: why did i do that?

Dearest Paige,

Don't be ridiculous. I was planning to write you a longer letter,
but my computer is running out of batteries. I'll recharge and
write or talk later. I hope that your dinner went well tonite.
Honest Abe.

I loved Lincoln. He was someone who made me feel more alive than I had ever hoped to feel. Fifteen minutes in his presence was a blessing. I said good-bye to him. I did not want to, but he needed to go. He was a live wire, and he conducted himself with precision, excess, finesse, and simple bodily ease. He was the captain. Oh,

19. Søren Kierkegaard, *Fear and Trembling / Repetition*, ed. and trans. Howard V. Hong and Edna H. Hong (Princeton, N.J.: Princeton University Press, 1983), p. 216.

Captain, my captain: the postmodern Abraham Lincoln. He was so alive and I felt so dead. He is probably the reason I got into e-mail trouble in the first place. He brought about in me a craving for more. For a time we corresponded, Abe and I, but the exchanges became less and less part of our daily lives. If I have to blame it on something, I blame it on Donna Tartt's *The Secret History*. *The Secret History* was involved in writing my life at this time. Upon returning to Williams I read the book. The story took place at a fictional college which stood in for Bennington, the nearby school up Route 7 in Vermont. It was about these students and this professor and death and tragedy and love and murder and class. It was a story about these students who were really smart and studied with a special professor. They want to realize the Greek texts he is teaching them in their daily lives, so they try to meet Dionysus. They end up killing a farmer in a moment of bacchanalia-induced frenzy, and then the plot unfolds. They are not found out initially; but later a character by the name of "Bunny" figures it out and begins to blackmail them. They decide that they have to escape or kill him. They kill him, and in the end it ruins every one of their lives. The teacher leaves the country.

My real relationship with Abe was based on honesty of a sort I have rarely encountered in my life. This relationship was tainted by gossip. Rumor is the stuff of the face-to-face community. I came to hate rumor and gossip. This episode killed it for me. E-mail looked better and better. Why did people talk about other people they knew? Why did so many people, including myself, whisper secrets that they told the listener not to repeat? I began to question myself seriously, to inspect myself for signs of pettiness. I hated that I had engaged in a secret history. I wanted no more secrets, lies, and confidences. I wanted light banter, and serious conversation.

I began to withdraw from everything and everyone. I felt guilty of a great sin. I wanted to be redeemed. I wondered and wondered and found no answers. I was alone, and needed to have my faith restored in the poetry of existence. What better place to look than in the wasteland?

STEP SEVEN:
*Humbly ask
God to remove
your sins.*

Act of Contrition

Most holy Mary, refuge of sinners,
I have offended in ways without number
thy Son whom thou lovest:
yet because He came to save sinners,
thou art the mother of sinners
who wish to repent. Receive me therefore,
assist me, and obtain for me the grace
of true and lasting contrition.[20]

Now I'm not saying that I killed anyone, or that any of my students did, as far as I know. What happened was that someone compared my Abraham Lincoln to Bunny. This was a moment in a long conversation, but it stuck. There were certain similarities, if you read him one way. I had never before read him that way. One night, after we had a long meal, I mentioned this comparison to him. He became enraged. He said he could no longer trust me. He hated rumors, and he hated that I had repeated this conversation. He left in a crash of rage and fury. I was horrified with myself. I had let fiction, metaphor, and rumor—the stuff of simulation—wound someone that I loved. I hated myself for doing it. I did it by accident, really, but once done the reason ceased to matter. It had been done. It was over. Now in hindsight, it wasn't Abraham that I was worried about losing at all. I was worried that I had lost my Emerson. Emerson had always been there for me, or so I had imagined. Suddenly, things began to happen where it was more and more difficult to talk to Emerson, and so I sought out other connections instead. I wish now that I had been better at talking at that time, but I was lost and confused. I was unsure of where I lived: my life was a secret history to myself. It had not always been that way.

20. Section of prayer made by John Hedley, Bishop in Wales for over thirty years, from *The Prayer Book: Beautiful and Helpful Prayers from Ancient and Modern Sources,* ed. Reverend John P. O'Connell and Jex Martin (Chicago: Catholic Press, 1954).

Perhaps a narrative would help here. It might give you, the reader, a sense of where I was at this time, and to do so I have to say something about where I'd been. I had returned from a leave at Harvard College, where I thought I would make connections. I did, but not where I wanted to initially. Some of these connections were about death; and others were about the abyss. Some of these connections were with the archives, where I found access to the handwritten journals of the heroines and heroes of my youth. I made connections with Louisa May Alcott; with Ralph Waldo Emerson; with Lydia Maria Child, and Margaret Fuller. They were all dead. I wanted to correspond with them.

Date: Thu, 27 Apr 1995 21:04:07 EDT
To: Multiple recipients of list <pscia@williams.edu>
From: A Student of politics
Subject: Re: Mary Wollstonecraft isn't Crazy.
Errors-To: s.paige.baty@williams.edu
Precedence: bulk

I decided to post my first message to the list server to respond to someone's observation that dealing with the objectification of women must go beyond simply recognizing that it exists and complaining about it to each other. A scientific inquiry into the motivations behind objectification would be useful and could lead to an eventual solution for the problem.

In the meantime, people should discourage objectification. It seems to me that the most effective way to do this is for women to stop conforming with the images that society says a woman should fit. If women didn't conform with what society says a woman should look/act like (i.e., thin, clothed in current fashion, passive, etc.), men would have to adapt. This adaptation might possibly be a restructuring of the parameters with which society (men) objectify women, but I hope instead it would destroy the objectification process. Perhaps, this is overly optimistic.

I want to stress that I'm not saying that it is the fault of women that they are objectified, or that it _should_ be their responsibility to change society. I am simply presenting the idea as the most pragmatic way to change current standards. To relate this to readings about minorities earlier in the semester, Martin Luther King and Malcolm X both observed that blacks couldn't wait for white society to change at its pace, so they had to encourage the pace. The oppressor generally doesn't stop oppression until the oppressed force them to. I realize that class differences and other social factors make unified action by women extremely difficult.

A final note is that I'm not trying to present an excuse for men to continue with their habits until women force them to change. Males should ideally participate in destroying the process, I just don't think that most will.

Is this logical? Accurate?

When I read the dead letters of the Alcotts I put thin white gloves on my hands and gingerly paged through old posted notes. I often had to strain my eyes to read the writing on the onion thin paper. I had to sign out these materials before I could read them. They did not arrive at my door, delivered by the mailman, to answer my address. They were all written to other dead people. I moved in Transcendentalist circles, spinning out pictures of lives now gone.

I went to Authors' Hill at a cemetery in Concord and visited my friends where our exchanges were made up of epitaphs: Emerson was especially prolific in having the final word on his dead family circle. The graves of the Alcotts were simply initials; these stone tablets were dwarfed by the monument to Emerson. I found solace in all of the graves, and the writing thereon, so I sat on a bench and waited to make a connection.

I wanted to have conversation with them in the way they had had conversations with one another; but I didn't even have a Ouija board as a way to make contact. I knew them: I had read their lives like books. I knew that for them conversation was a way of life. They wrote and spoke constantly. They were always involved in the process of making themselves up.

I wanted to make myself up in conversations with others. One of the first places I tried was the library; the second was the burial ground. These places were not so different as it might seem. Each was a repository of life-writing. In the library the life-writing was about excess: in the graveyard it took the form of moderation. In the library there were tomes, in the graveyard there were tombs.

I thought a lot about the body of the text. In the library it was about content; in the graveyard it was human form. It was cold in the graveyard and I felt more and more alone. Everyone I was talking to was dead. Footnotes and headstones began to blur for me. I had spent my whole life in school, and now I had landed in a graveyard filled with those I'd been making a study of. I saw them as friends, but there were simply things they could not do for me: it was all one-way exchanges. I could bring them flowers, but I would not receive the same. I could write them poetry, send them valentines, take pictures of their tombstones, but we couldn't have a conversation.

I kept talking anyway, but I wanted more. This is my sin: I wanted more too often.

Date: Thurs., 02 Feb. 1995 17:55:07 PST
To: "Dr. Rocket" <S.Paige.Baty@williams.edu>
From: Live Wire
Subject: Re: the quick and the tedious

On Feb. 2, 7:58pm, Dr. Rocket wrote:

> Subject: Re: i only have spam for you
>
> So are you going to respond to me or do we do the same dance
> again? I know you read your e-mail. Me, I'm some crazy fe-mail
> teaching little bits of wisdom to everyone but myself. Still, I try,
> or at least I know you know I'm trying. Thought I'd give you that
> one. Today they gave me a Powermac 7100 so I am psyched. I
> am becoming computer literati. Nice. Or as my friend would say,
> "Sweet, dude." Sweets for the sweet. I suffer from schizophelia.
> I love women who love poetry and death but I secretly want to
> be Shakespeare. Help. "Looking for brilliant German academician
> who predicts death of god and writes immortal theory in hotels
> during three week stay. Must love long walks and neurotic, self-
> obsessed fellow would-be immortal. Must like clean floors.
> Sense of humor a must. No hippies or rational choice theorists
> need apply. Tolerance a necessity. Hey, but all of the interesting
> people are the difficult ones, right? Yeah, sure Spage.
>
> -- End of excerpt from Dr. Rocket

What? Wasn't spam enough?

Oh great, my worst nightmare: a semi-computer-literate spaige in sigh-ber-space.

Spam is an anagram for maps. One of the great regrets in my life is that my lover and I did not take the time to visit the Spam museum. Now that time is over, but I would like it back. So much of living is about looking back and seeing how you could have done things differently. But where will this way of living take us? It seems greedy not simply to be satisfied with what we have had. Especially, those of us who have been given so much. We are rarely content with what we have known. We want more. Why is it that we so often ask for more? Second helpings, more money, more understanding, more and more from those we know?

I wanted more, and I wanted to know more, and I wanted to make connections. I lived in a world surrounded by ghosts, and I was haunted by their specters. Sure, I had the tools: books, journals, letters, the houses they lived in; but I couldn't have them. I wanted to know them too well. Dead people expect very little: they are happy with a poem, a flower, the simple speaking of their name. Yet they, too, became demanding, as I was painted awash in their flow between being and non-being. They were my vampire friends. They took me into their sepulchers. I felt more and more bone than flesh and blood. I read the endings of books first. I saw in the bloom of the rose its inevitable ending. Teleologies were re-versing my life. I spent more and more time at the library. I was buried in the past. I began to feel I had joined the silent ranks of the dead. Being and time are unwritten by the dead. They, too, were unwriting me. QUESTION: was it poetic or pathetic? Eros or pathos?

Eros and pathos make up romance in our culture. When I wasn't in the library or at the cemetery I rode around in my car. The radio was filled with paeans to lost love, or the possibilities of love everlasting. I listened to the "Oldies" channel and I began to feel old. Songs that were new when I was a child were now the stuff of a common cultural memory; time passed. Me, I was stuck in time.

I knew that I, too, was dying. The music, the flowers, the picnics, the fireflies would all pass. I wrote on the slate in my cramped quarters at Lowell House, "This too shall Pass." The chalk crumbled in my hand. I was stuck in the mire of endings, O, but my heart longed for beginnings.

Date: Wed, 05 Apr. 1995 21:32:48 EDT
To: S.Paige.Baty@williams.edu
From: Goethe
Subject: Re: My favorite, myself

Dear Paige:

Thanks for your letter and especially for the poetry.

You know, I had some second thoughts after sending my letter out, but then realized that you seemed not only like someone who appreciates honesty but also someone who can take things said straight out even if awkwardly expressed and seemingly critical. So I appreciate your response. I didn't mean (re: one thought at a time) to try to censor you, or even think that I could persuade you to slow down for my benefit. You are who you are. And I like people who are high energy and like to burn it at both ends. I've been looking forward to meeting you since I read one of the e-mail excerpts from what you sent to Thomas Aqua Vitae

To respond to some of your letter:

> Look. we are adults so we can compromise, but i never
> compromise myself.

Cool.

> I am sorry it was one sided. sometimes i never talk.
> Lately i talk a lot because i feel a sense of urgency and I am not
> sure why.
> Just if i am too fast tell me to slow down and i will try and do it.
> It hurts my feelings that you felt it was one-sided. i liked you
> when we spoke.

Sorry about hurting your feelings. But all I was doing was being who I am and telling you what I felt. Thanks for your invitation to ask you to slow down; I guess that's all I was getting at anyway --giving myself some space to say so. (Very west coast thing to say; even juiced up on espresso as I am at the moment, I'm still psychologically mellow.) Also, so you know, I feel I express myself better when I'm writing.

> i want to know more about you.

Just ask. Oh, you did.

> what your days are like?

Mostly I sit in my office and either (1) talk on the telephone or (2) type stuff on the computer. Yet I love the work. I don't like the telephone stuff that much, which has increased quite a bit since I've been promoted to Litigation Director (people call me asking for jobs, advice, etc.). I do like talking to clients on the phone and doing on the spot problem solving, which is a huge piece of my job.

It's a long, complicated answer. I'll save it for in-person. It is a fluid answer, and changes as I change. I came into it for certain (romantic, sentimental) reasons; I stay in it for some of the same reasons, but also for other, harder nosed reasons having to do with my own politics, emotions, and sense of enjoyment.

> what is your vision?

Save for later.

> why can't you commit in relationships?

Good question. If I knew the answer, I might be able to figure out how to commit. I like the concept, dislike the practice (so far; maybe, as my mom tells me, I just haven't met "the right one." Whatever.)

> why did you feel i talked too fast or too much?

Because I felt like I only was able to process about a third of what you were saying. I would be responding to one thought in my head and you would be two or three concepts down the line on me.

>does that scare you?

I used to be east coast, lots faster, and can get into that mode if I have to. One thing that I have learned in spending time with Native peoples is the value of silence, of not answering right away, of putting one's thoughts together, of letting the thoughts tumble around each other until they come together. In fact, one of the first things I had to learn when i started working here was to stop talking and start listening a lot harder, noticing the non-verbal cues when a tribal person was going to speak or wasn't yet done speaking. And its a valuable thing that I like to do. I can go word for word with you (all previous false modesty aside), and will at times, if i'm feeling like it. But I don't always like to. And like you, i like my solitudes and silences. Also, I wonder if a person who's talking real fast is really in a conversation and wants to hear what the other person wants to say or only wants to say what's on their mind and is not that interested in the other (damn that's an awkward sentence but I'll leave it that way to prove some kind of point or another).

> because i will tell you i am a very strong person

I can sense as much, but one never can tell. I enjoy being around strong people. I do wonder about the sense of urgency you feel. I sometimes feel that way too, and it usually expresses itself in insomnia. Although unlike you, I don't get anything done, just lay around in the dark and imagine the worst case scenario of whatever's on my mind. Maybe I should get out of bed and follow your example and do shit. (Whoops, there's that scatological stuff again.) But then I'll be too tired to do my work the next day, and my work is my life's priority.

> i'm not so one-sided really.

I didn't mean to imply that YOU were one-sided. Just the opposite. You seem quite multifaceted; I was just asking for the time to process it all. If you simply spoke fast but said garbage, I wouldn't care how fast you talked because I wouldn't need to listen. I know lots of people like that. But you say stuff that is worth hearing and thinking about.

It does seem to me like i might have hit a sore spot, and i'm sorry if i did so unthinkingly. I certainly don't want to get things off on the wrong foot with you. It appears that you still want to correspond with me, so i'm assuming any damage done has been minor. I intend to remain honest and forthright with you, and will try to put things in the "I-feel" mode.

Later,
The Good man

P.S. Whatever.

I wandered Boston alone. I came upon the memorial to Mary Baker Eddy at the Christian Science center. I read in their literature that she had a phone installed in her grave, and that it was operable. I tried, without success, to get her number. Calling upon the dead was no easy matter. Nonetheless, I wrote them letters which I called books to try and breathe some life into their tired forms. But the more I wrote, the less I believed in my audience: who would read these books? I didn't even know them. I wanted to have written and spoken exchanges with someone that I knew, but as the year dwindled to a close, this seemed less and less possible. I have the phone bills to prove it; I wanted to talk to someone who knew me. Still, the calls were unsettling. I hated giving reports on my life, because I was unsure at that time where I lived, or what I was doing.

REPETITION: KIERKEGAARD

*Some time went by . . . At certain times, like Emperor Domitian,
I even walked around the room armed with a flyswatter, pursuing
every revolutionary fly. Three flies, however, were preserved to
fly buzzing through the room at specified times. Thus did I live,
forgetting the world and, as I thought, forgotten, when one day
a letter arrived from my young friend. More followed, always
spaced about a month apart, but from this I dared not draw any
conclusion as to the distance of his place of residence. He himself
divulges nothing, and he could very well be trying to perplex me
by deliberately and carefully varying the intervals between five
weeks and just a day over three weeks. He does not wish to
trouble me with a correspondence, and even if I were willing to
reciprocate or at least to answer his letters, he does not care to
receive anything like that—he simply wishes to pour himself out.*[21]

21. Kierkegaard, *Fear and Trembling / Repetition,* pp. 179–180. *Note:* this book will be repeatedly sampled throughout the text, as was the way of Søren and as is the way of Norman O. Brown and as was the way of Roland Barthes. This book is a re-wiring of all of their work, especially *Love's Body, Repetition, Barthes by Barthes,* and *Camera Lucida.* Kierkegaard wrote under pseudonyms, pre-figuring dead authors and e-mail. Barthes wrote a form of autobiography and poetry as theory. Brown was a cut-and-paste man. I reassemble their forms in this text.

In the e-mail world people pour themselves out as virtual characters. These characters are both letters and names. Sometimes, however, these people attend real-life parties. Racer X told me the story of one such party he attended at the University on the Hill. All of the self-named "Geeks" were there. A couple of other people, who were not on line, attended the party. They had no pseudonyms. They had not hung out in a MUD or a Chat Room with the other virtual characters. At the party the virtual characters all called one another by their pseudonyms. The people at the party who had no virtual life were referred to as "people of no account." This was the common vernacular of this culture. It was based on puns, the Internet, and a ruthless mentality. People who lived in the virtual world knew how to swat flies: they made them into "people of no account." Repetition and pleasure were the name of the game. The name game.

I imagine myself as a guest at this party. I am Bunny, and it is *Who's Afraid of Virginia Woolf?* This is an academic exercise. This is a zoo story. This is a story about cities of circuitry. You have to be in the game to play. You need a name to play. You live in a world where you play games with naming. Maybe you think you have an imaginary son. You give him a history. You play the game again and again. One day, you confront the real, abruptly. Someone kills your imaginary son. You don't know why it happened. Wait, did I say I was Bunny? Maybe I was Martha? Maybe I was the young professor. Maybe I was Edward Albee. Maybe I was Elizabeth Taylor. Maybe I was the failed professor. Maybe I was Alice, down the bunny hole.

Games, Albee, and Virginia Woolf. The whole game was shot on location at Smith College, where I went to school. Who was afraid then? Not I, said the student I used to be. At that time I had picnics on the lawn in front of the house where they shot that movie. That edifice loomed, complex, behind me and the other young women with whom I lived. We mostly ignored it. We mostly had picnics, and went to parties, and pulled "all-nighters" writing our papers. We didn't speak often of Virginia Woolf, but we knew about her. We were in a place that was built by women like her, or was made possible by women like her. We were not afraid of Virginia Woolf. We called each other by our real names: Jo, Meg, Amy, and Beth. Or was it Heidi and Jo and Sarah and Katherine? I was the little Princess in that name game: Sarah. I never used that name: Sarah Paige. I know what Abraham almost did to Sarah's son. Still, the name means, "one who laughs." I laughed a lot in those days, but I cried a lot too. I had read my Sylvia Plath. I knew how I had come to Smith.

Date: Mon., 13 Feb. 1995 15:39:32 EST
To: S.Paige.Baty@williams.edu
From: grindstoned
Subject: i couldn't

find your homepaige

i looked and looked and couldn't find

your home, page

bye

I had moved constantly. I left Birmingham, Alabama, when I was very young when my family relocated to San Francisco. In California

I moved several times. I left California, land of my youth, for North-ampton, Massachusetts, where I received my undergraduate degree from Smith College. I then moved back to California, where I received my doctorate at the University of California at Santa Cruz. I had a series of job interviews around the country. One of these was at my favorite dream of a future: Berkeley. As fate would have it, I didn't end up in the enchanted halls of the University I had visited as a child. I had an interview there, and some people were mad, or said I was. One man tried to insult me in the privacy of his office. "You," he said, "should write fiction." He was no Prince Charming: he fought dragons of feminism and lesbianism and postmodernism and any old ism, I guess. I tried to charm him by being a good daughter. I took his suggestions with a mock-turtleneck serious air: "you should see how many Republicans versus Democrats care about Marilyn Monroe," he told me. I said it made an interesting point. He shook my hand and I walked away.

This is a fairy tale, told late into the evening. Now, I wish I'd battled that dragon that day, but I did not. I am, however, happy to say that what to him was an insult I took as a compliment and a statement about the nature of reality: it's all a strange fiction. If there is one thing you learn as a professor it's *Discipline and Punish*, or maybe the meaning of *Power/Knowledge*. I know why Foucault is so popular among professors: he wrote our autobiographies, or maybe I should say, he was a good ethnographer. This is also why people are so afraid of him. He wasn't afraid of writing, talking, and living. He made some mistakes, but who among you has not? I have, and I am no Michel Foucault.

THE DEAD AUTHOR SPEAKS

In a book ironically entitled *Foucault Live*, the dead author is asked:

Q: The Archeology of Knowledge *announced a forthcoming* History of Sexuality. *The next volume appeared eight years later and according to a plan completely different.*

MF: I changed my mind. A work, when it's not at the same time an attempt to modify what one thinks and even what one is, is not much fun. I had begun to write two books in accordance with my original plan; but very quickly I got bored. It was unwise on my part and contrary to my habits.

Q: Then why did you do it?

MF: Out of laziness. I dreamed that a day would come when I would know in advance what I meant and would only have to say it. That was a reflection of old age. I imagined I had finally reached the age when one only has to reel out what's in one's head. It was both a form of presumption and an abandonment of restraint. Yet to work is to undertake to think something other than what one has thought before.

Q: The reader thought so too.

MF: With respect to the reader, I feel at the same time certain qualms and a fair amount of confidence. The reader is like an auditor of a course. He can easily tell when one has worked and when one merely talks off the top of one's head. He may be disappointed, but not by the fact that I have said nothing else but what I was already saying.[22]

Back to the classroom, only let's call it the story for the sake of the plot. You, reader, are the auditor in this course. I am reeling off what is in my head, and I'm writing two books at once. Presumption and abandonment inform this text: you may be disappointed, but not by the fact that I have said nothing other than what I was already saying. It's all about repetition. We spend most of our lives telling other people the story of our lives. We spend most of our lives making up stories. This is a story. You can always drop the class, if you want to.

22. Michel Foucault, *Foucault Live (Interviews 1961–1984)*, ed. Sylvère Lotringer; trans. Lysa Hochroth and John Johnston (New York: Semiotext(e) Double Agents Series, 1996), p. 455.

Date: Wed, 08 Feb. 1995 00:12:20 EST
To: S.Paige.Baty@williams.edu
From: The Sub-Letter
Subject: i called

i called
i called
i called
i did my laundry
i fell asleep reading habermas
i am stupid
i will never be as smart as you
i cannot read as fast as you
i called
i am a callous friend
maybe that makes me no friend at all

Going to school, professing, helps you to grow callous, or to grow hard parts on the soft edges of your feet you never thought you'd find. But there they are, when you are taking a bath, and you scrub them off. You learn to get rid of dead skin. You become a snake in the garden. You offer the promise of knowledge; maybe you live for it. It's all a trick. You are tricking yourself and others into believing that certain forms of knowledge will save them, or help them know something they need to know to make their marks, to live up to the grade. This knowledge alone cannot save you. There are so many things I "know," but this does not necessarily change the ways I act and react to situations. I learned to know in a way that was often apart from myself. I learned to succeed at certain things, but that success did not bring me happiness, or solace, or love, or peace. It just brought me more deadlines and more of a need to succeed. At a certain point I was no longer sure who I was performing for, or what success meant to me. At this point standards became blurry. Who was my audience? Was I writing and performing for the people I knew, for the people I'd grown up with, or for some weird thing called "posterity" where true success would grant me immortality? Could I find a true "audience" in another soul?

Souls are not often discussed in the places I have lived these past years. I have lived primarily in school. I found myself in my thirties having never left for so much as a recess. My life was made up of a series of tests. I took them all, and I have kept on taking them. I graduated from high school. I got my bachelor's degree. I passed my orals, and found my masters. I wrote a dissertation and received a Ph.D. I then went "on the market," which is another test. Interviews were tests that read both ways: they read me and I read them back. Now I am writing back to you, and telling you that I will no longer take your tests; and I will not inflict them on anybody else. I've been scared sacred, scarred but not lamed. I picked up my stick and kept on walking. Remember, Oedipus did it. It's all about the journey. At a certain point a soul chooses the tests she will take, or make up herself. If she cannot do this, then she cannot go on with her life. She is stuck in someone else's narrative.

I have reached that point in the journey where I have rejected the structures that bid me, however compellingly, to do as I ought in order to be some vision of what a woman and soul is supposed to be in our time. But I wasn't always here, and that's why there is a narrative, or some semblance of one, in the first place. "I resemble that remark," someone said over my shoulder in El Rio yesterday around eight o'clock. I liked the comment, and repeated it to Ruth. "I've heard it before," she told me; "everyone around here says it." I still liked it anyway. Originality is not my standard of invention, communication, or honesty. The further I went into school the more the entire concept of "origin" became tainted for me. Still, I looked for origin stories that would make sense of how I had come to be, and how everything around me had come to be. This is the thinker's curse: she wants an answer to everything. Maybe sometimes there are simply no answers, or there are no simple answers. Sometimes thinking may mean giving up on answers. Perhaps this is when thinking marries being. Then maybe there can be a life where the two are not separate but each parts of the same, making up the whole of a life for a time, or a woman, or a country, or a system of communication. Otherwise we are left with phantoms, and these phantoms do not lead you to a place of peace and belonging: they simply leave you with more and more longings.

Re:semblance of a life. Back to the story: the back story. I got a one-year job and packed up some of my belongings like a pioneer woman or hobo headed west, but backwards. I didn't know what the future would bring. Among the things I couldn't pack were my favorite dishes, Christmas ornaments, and my boyfriend of five years. He was going to Encino to sell life insurance. What a curious thing: there are no such guarantees, but people buy it anyway. For most things there is no assurance, much less insurance: within the year I lost the dishes, the ornaments, and the boyfriend. I miss him still. He was baggage I should not have left behind, but I did not yet know what losing someone meant. I thought I'd always be okay. I was wrong, but then again, in the big picture I was right. I had come to think of myself as this portable unit able to live, write, and work despite everything that happened around me. Now, I am much less movable. Movement seemed an inevitability. And so I became my own company and I left my lover for a dream of a life I would live. It was part of the skin-shedding I had come to associate with knowledge. This meant leaving community, and treating oneself as the ultimate company. Labour lost me my loves: Love/Labour's Lost. But oh I did so believe that I wanted to go into labor that I swapped a life by the ocean filled with redwood trees and poppies for a life in the purple mountains filled with birches and history. It wasn't a bad trade, but it was a big change of location for the plot.

```
Date:     Sat, 04 Feb. 1995 12:45:42 EST
To:       S.Paige.Baty@williams.edu
From:     Speedy
Subject:  where are you?

what are you doing?
i keep passing you like a signal on crossed wires.
want to hang out and work and cook and kill time in this snow
storm with you and co. and maybe my co. but not your co. because
your co. is a real Inc. co.
Well, i hope i run into you EVENTUALLY. I call often, but you can
call me Al
```

STEP SIX:
*Be ready to
have God
remove these
defects of
character.*

It seemed that everyone was missing me while I found myself missing everyone I loved. Still, I believed in happily-ever-afters. I believed in the trade. I believed in decency, integrity, loyalty, honesty, and all of the other things my family and teachers had brought me up to believe in. I thought that if I played the game the fair way, it didn't matter who would win or lose. In sum, in the aftermath of it all, each player played by different rules. I had to stake out some other territory if I was to make it through this matrix. I fought as I was born again and again, even while I was stuck learning the same lessons. I ended up with the birth that is now myself. Still, I hold dear those who brought me up and the values they instilled in me.

```
Date:     Sun, 15 Jan 1995 15:31:08 EST
To:       S.Paige.Baty@williams.edu
From:     starsky
Subject:  battie

you sound truly happy
i hope you are. if not,
or if so, let me know,
so i can go and get you
a copy of friday's NY POST
which reads: paraphrased:
Simpson Shocked By Race Issue
(no joke, it really is like that)
```

THE PLOT QUICKENS

I left Santa Cruz for Williamstown, Massachusetts, where I was to be a visiting assistant professor. Initially, I had a one-year appointment with liberal arts education, but the institution took me in. I became one of them for awhile. I spent every summer away from Williamstown, in different parts of the country. My life felt very mobile, and I suppose that this offered a sort of freedom. Still, I spent a lot of my time packing up my clothes and books and moving between different places. I never bought a plant for fear it would require too great a commitment. Other people often lived in my apartment when I was gone, and so I'd clear off my things to make space for them. I was always choosing. Choosing what clothing I needed for what climate I'd live in; choosing which books I required for what I was writing; choosing which dishes and towels to pack for fear that a sub-letter would break some precious keepsake. I always had to decide what to pack tight and shut away from a stranger who would live among the collection of furniture, pictures, and dishes that made up my life. And when I lived somewhere else, I was in a constant state of flux, eating off of someone else's dishes, sleeping on someone else's bed. I was not sure where I lived anymore. The only thing that was constant was the work, and a dream of a future when everything would resolve itself in a happy ending, and I would finally inhabit the world I lived in. I didn't know where I lived anymore, so I stopped living altogether.

SOME MORE DISPATCHES

Flying over jungle was almost pure pleasure, doing it on foot was nearly all pain. I never belonged in there. Maybe it really was what its people had always called it, Beyond; at the very least it was serious, I gave up things to it I probably never got back.[23]

I feel a warm correspondence with this man who went to cover the war in Viet Nam. I love Herr's dispatches with a passion. In one passage I feel he is speaking to me. He tells the story of a commander who comes upon him and another man covering the war, "Page." The commander is upset when he passes and they don't salute.

"Don't you men salute officers?"
"We're not men," Page said, "We're correspondents."[24]

Exactly, mein Herr: we're not men; we're correspondents. I am writing this dispatch to you from another jungle. Here the blood is not so easily seen, and the body count isn't as high. But there is a war going on, and I am a correspondent although I sometimes feel like a foot soldier.

23. Herr, *Dispatches*, p. 10.

24. Ibid., p. 7.

We had at Williams the great honor and luxury of a year-and-a-half leave after only three years of teaching, providing that we got matching grants. It was for this reason that I had landed on the steps of Widener Library at Harvard, where I had received a Mellon Fellowship. I moved once more, this time to Cambridge in rented quarters surrounded by students. I tried to make a home in two small rooms at Lowell House, but found that I couldn't. I got out of my rooms whenever I could. Everyone and everything felt so temporary: each new relationship I entered was one I'd have to leave in a few months. I made a couple of very good friends there, but kept mostly to myself and my dead authors. Sometimes my old friends would visit me. Many of them were also in a state of flux; or they had moved to places like Miami, Oberlin, Oakland, San Diego, even Transylvania, Kentucky. I lived in a world of shifting tectonic plates: The word "home" dropped out of my vocabulary.

After a year at Harvard, a "professional on leave," I went to Minneapolis to live with my lover. I was a professional "on leave" and I had to make choices: so much freedom of choice. But everywhere I went meant that I didn't go someplace else, and all those missed places were missing family and people and trees and lakes I would come to love for a time, or that I've continued loving. Love, land, and separation all seemed to come together and apart at the same time. A week at a cabin in Luck, Wisconsin. There I came to love a particular muskrat that swam by the docks at dawn, on a regular schedule, as if to greet me. I sat alone on the dock and stared at the stars. What stars were the people I loved seeing? We moved in separate constellations of thought, time, and space: a thousand and one points of night, never staying too long with one person or another. It seemed to be about mobility, but I was not moved. I just moved around.

(This, too, is female trouble for the career woman. Very few men relocate to live with a lover who takes a job somewhere else. This is true in the academy, and true in many other "white-collar" professions. Most of the women I knew who were professors commuted somewhere else to see their partners; whereas almost every man I knew had a wife or girlfriend who had moved to be with him. If people were in same-sex relationships, the rules seemed to vary a bit more, but not entirely. And, of course, there are exceptions to every rule. I knew a handful of women who had partners who had moved to live with them, some gay and some straight. Still, the name of the game was usually the male man moved and the woman followed, and made a home for him. Home-making and female trouble are linked, just as searching for community and e-mail trouble are linked. Nonetheless, I saw an awful lot of disconnection, what Lewis Carroll called "Logical Nonsense," played out in this game of cultural chess.

Check:mates? What do you call yourself, married or single? What if you are in a same-sex relationship? What if you are divorced? What if you are engaged? What if you see several people? What if your world keeps changing? How do you fit into the forms that you fill out with and as your life?)

Where were we, or where was I? Oh, yes, in Minneapolis, Minnesota: land of 10,000 lakes. For my lover's sake, I tried my hand at living in a city where I knew virtually no one. I didn't want to meet too many people because I would only be there for a few months. I tried to make a home out of a high-rise apartment with its own deli and liquor store and found that I couldn't do it. The apartment complex was large, stylish, and dead. I passed people I didn't know in elevators. I walked on silent carpets to the garbage chute. I ate prepared food from the deli. I went out alone at night. The city was freezing by November; and so it was no small task to get out of my beehive of a house. There were no good libraries or graveyards to visit. I was homesick; although I wasn't sure where home was, I knew it wasn't here. I did not understand the Midwest, and this was its cultural Mecca. I was a pilgrim lost, yearning for Plymouth Rock or something bigger and better upon which I could build a foundation for myself. Many are the ways to number the conditions of the homeless in our times.

Date: WE, 11 Jan 1995 00"34:46 EST
To: Paige Baty <S. Paige Baty@williams.edu>
From: Solid As a Rock
Subject: Re: pol. theory

Is this e-mail correspondence impractical?
should I call or stop by?
(I guess if the first is true the next two become rhetorical)

In the middle passage of this period I went to California and lived a happy life for a month. I decided to stay, but was drawn back by the ties that had me bound. In two more months I was back in my apartment in Williamstown. It was a relief, but I seemed to be living in lodging quarters again. I unpacked my belongings, and realized that I had been living out of boxes and suitcases for a year and a half. I set about the task of making altars in my home. My tools were wax grapes, Fiesta ware, pictures of the Virgin, and old books. For color and salvation I added Catholic prayer candles, with tints purple, golden, lime, and red. I lit these at night as I returned to my dead authors. I hated television, and found that the sight of it made me sick. (I had watched too much of *The Real World* too many times in Minnesota.) The apartment was filled with the detritus of sub-letters who had lived in my home when I was "on leave." I was constantly running into remainders of someone else's life: a child's sticker on my living room wall—a purple ink mark on my kitchen floor. These were the traces the strangers had left me, in addition to other marks of common ruin. Once the couple living there had flooded the kitchen after failing to properly install a rented washing machine. Now the paint on the walls was peeling up to three feet off the floor. My neighbors told me the phone lines had gone out in the building for a week. The whole complex was off line.

Where was I? Oh yes, back at school. I began teaching once more; only this time I was teaching a winter term class using a book I'd written on Marilyn Monroe and cultural memory. The students were bright, enthusiastic, and young. They asked me questions about myself, especially about a footnote early on in the book that puzzled them: Was their teacher hidden in there?

6. As such, it is a schizophrenic text, and this is reflected in the voices of its author. I have been listening for some time to the voices of those who have made the goddess, the chroniclers of mass-mediated immortality. What I have heard is the static of the airwaves, something that runs interference over the story that is told again and again. This listening has been the act of making

Marilyn, and it has meant living with her, or the version of her I was writing. Everybody's Marilyn is different. My Marilyn sits at the nexus of academia and my television screen, the crossroads where I stand unable to make that terrible decision to kill, unknowingly, the father. So this crossroads doubles into the space where I have met the sphinx of Marilyn and her suicide, a monstrous female that keeps asking me and itself, "How does it end? What does it mean?" There have been no one-line answers to this riddled identity, but I have thought about the question as a way of beginning to answer it. I decided to live on the outskirts of the plague-ridden city and to talk for a while to this terrible sphinx, remembering patriarchy back at the first crossroads, the ones that led me to the gates of the city. I prefer to think of this experience as theory in exile, in a place where exile is a kind of involvement, a way of staying engaged by watching and talking from the gates—outside, but almost in. This is what I will think of as Marilyn country. Inhabiting "Marilyn country" requires a productive schizophrenia, a state Norman Mailer understands quite well. For Marilyn refuses the simple dichotomies of fact and fiction, fantasy and history, as she is made up over the years, and even as she made herself up during her lifetime.[25]

The students examined their teacher carefully. Was she saying that she was a schizophrenic? The students did not know the Oedipus myth, so they didn't see what I meant by crossroads and patriarchy. They wanted to know if I meant that I wanted to kill myself or my father. (I could not kill him: he had died six months earlier in New Orleans.) The students had found a new game: solving the riddle of their teacher. I was their sphinx, and my questions about the book they interpreted as riddles. They were my sphinx, and their questions about the book seemed posed by gatekeepers. They were so young to be keeping gates. They were impressed with the fact that I knew so much about television, but I didn't have the heart to confess I hadn't turned it on in months. It had exhausted me.

I wanted to go, at least for a year or two, to that place that is looking backwards. Not to the side did I look; not to the future, but

25. Baty, *American Monroe*, p. 27.

to the past and present. This was my all-too-human condition. I was searching for something, and at that time I didn't know what it was. Now I do. I was searching for what Hannah Arendt calls the two great human faculties: forgiveness and the ability to make promises.[26] How could I do this when I was stuck between past and future? I was a missing person getting messages from people I didn't know well enough to miss. Get the net? I thought I'd find my face on some milk carton. Maybe then I could go home.

Date: Wed, 26 Apr. 1995 18:04:11 EDT
To: S.Paige.Baty@williams.edu
From: The Good Man
Subject: Re: Latest Odds

Dear Spaige:

Promises, promises.

Thanks so much for the words of comfort and encouragement, they were (and are) much needed.

By the way, I read Neal's e-mail re: hoops and one-on-one and didn't think it was strange at all. Rather, it was a guy way of saying "I'm looking forward to seeing you and spending some time with you and that means a lot to me." You need to brush up on guyspeak, especially regarding the sharing of affection.

Don't worry. Be happy.
Affectionately,

The Good Man

If only things had been so simple. This was not the first time I had received a message with the words "Don't Worry, Be Happy" on it. In a *real* letter from one of my best friends I had received the same message years before. I still have that letter. He had found a small yellow card with a picture of "Meher Baba" imprinted with the words, "Don't Worry. Be Happy." In this letter my friend wrote to me:

26. Hannah Arendt, *The Human Condition* (Chicago: University of Chicago Press, 1958). See discussion on pp. 236–247.

Sarah Paige Sarah Paige!! I won't even pretend to
spell the last name. Welcome to the world of wellness.
We expect you to stay, so don't sneak away and Lay or
is it Lie on your side. This very second all choice has been denied.
    I have the
Prescription. YA!

I am alone in my room, you are asleep in yours. I feel
close to you there; (Do people who are in love ever make
those famous comments on what they think love is?
or is it the frustrated ones who can't decide whether
it's a state, a condition, a sickness, an inadequacy, or a
    passion . . .)
parenthetical lighter than air. it will float or
already has five feet above my presence and popped.

Q: When I'm not there do you face the wall? . . .
today thinking of you in morning Sunday nontraffic
in the middle of the street, I was smiling and watching
the nonhappenings all over town. a pleasant fade back
to school. energy flow was fluent, I knew the vibes were
fine. I found this card. I knew why cosmo was speaking
so loudly. 1) Meher Baba never kids around. 2) The paper
I was carrying is faded perfectly with the card and 3)
He has a trick forehead like you. But his is trickier because
his hairline recedes. Meher speaks a clean mess-age.
Thinking of you and being with you rubs me this way.
I appreciate pretty much a lot of stuff about you. You
are worth 20x every small difficult moment there may be.
I respect those moments as you do. As we surmount them,
now in a much more vaulting rather than trudging fashion;
I don't know what I was saying and it's no fair to look onto
the other side. I miss you very much right now and love you
always. Yourfriendlovercompanionxxxxxx

Don't Worry. Be Happy. Why could I never seem to get that message down? As it turned out I did not turn my back on worry;

although I knew at many times great happiness. But that happiness was also countered with a spell of discontent that even my keen analytic mild could not rend. I wanted to find solace, to be content. I was to go on a long mazed journey where I'd face my own fire to search for these things, and still, I am implicated in the labyrinth I was lost in. I wanted so much. I wanted answers and love and guarantees. I wanted to correspond with someone, and to know that it would last, now and forever even unto the end of time. I was to learn that forever guarantees did not, on the whole, exist. Maybe with cars and washing machines and computers there are guarantees, but there is no insurance of life itself. This was something no one could give me; oh, but how I wanted it. Was it love or immortality I sought?

NOTE INTERRUPTS THE PLOT. I get a letter addressed simply to "Paige" from Silicon Studios. It is a forwarded message you get from wraith@netcom. The message reads like this:

to invite someone dangerous to tea;
to make friends with freedom and uncertainty;
to look forward to dreams;
to cry during movies; to swing as high as I can on a swingset, by moonlight;
to cultivate moods;
to refuse to "be responsible";
to do it for love;
to take lots of naps;
to make little signs that say "yes!" and post them all over my house;
to give money away;
to do it now;
to know the money will follow;
to believe in magic;
to laugh a lot;
to celebrate every gorgeous moment;
to have wild imaginings;
to have transformative dreams;
to have perfect calm;
to draw on the walls;
to read everyday;
to imagine myself magic;
to giggle with children;

to listen to old people;
to open up;
to dive in;
to be free;
to bless myself;
to drive away fear;
to play with everything;
to entertain my inner child;
to build a fort with blankets;
to hug trees;
to write love letters;
to plant impossible gardens.

Who is wraith@netcom.com? Why did he or she leave this Post-it Note of an advertisement for himself on the Web? It reads like a cross between a personals ad and a bad lesson in Buddhism. But maybe there are no bad lessons in Buddhism. If you meet Buddha on the road: kill him. Is this the real lesson? Or was the note about longing and immortality and a thirst for poetry and the real? Did the person you contact when you fingered the wraith want to find a true love on the Internet? Was he singing his body, electric? I did not know.

I wondered if he had recently attended the Forum, and they had given him this advice. I wondered if he really gave money away freely. I imagined his apartment, filled with yellow Post-it Notes that shouted, "Yes!" I imagined him or maybe her swinging with me on the swingset at Trace Elementary School in San Jose where Barbara Noir and I swung in our flannel nightgowns as hard and high and fast as we could every time we snuck out of her house at night, away from her Mormon parents' watchful eyes. We loved that playground at a school called "Trace Elementary."

In a way Wraith was describing Barbara's and my world. We lived in a Barbie-doll of a reality we played for years, with characters good and bad who got dressed and drove their shoeboxes to work and had names like Bubbles and Barbie and Tracy and Skipper and Janet and oh so many more. These dolls had dark relationships with one another. All they did was fall in and out of love and life. They screamed and fought. We played out their lives every day after school as long and hard and fast as we could. We wrote each other letters about them. We each kept journals, and in these our dolls also lived.

We grew up together, two girls who imagined ourselves magic, celebrating every gorgeous San Jose Moment; giggling, playing with everything. We were are own inner children, because we were children. So, Barbara, we were children together. And now we are grown up: women.

The thing is the story with Barbara has a happy ending. We are still best friends. She invites me to her house and we play piano, and sing songs, like "Sunrise/Sunset." We remember when we entered the sixth-grade talent show and lost to the tap-dancing girl whose mother had made her a star-spangled suit that let her tap-tap-tap to the record spinning backstage. When she won we were enraged. We believed our song had so much more pathos. We still do. It does. We did not end up broken, over, and off line. We talk and connect and see each other all the time. Maybe the Wraith is looking for his childhood playmates. Maybe for awhile I forgot all the good in my friends. I didn't know then what I know now: I already had everything I needed anyway. No one was going to give it to me except the people I already knew: the lonesome traveler always went home to write books. Part of what it took to soothe him was his mother, and his other kin.

JACK KEROUUUACCC HAS NEW YORK SCENES AT HOME

At this time my mother was living alone in a little apartment in Jamaica Long Island, working in the shoe factory, waiting for me to come home so I could keep her company and escort her to Radio City once a month. She had a tiny bedroom waiting for me, clean linen in the dresser, clean sheets in the bed. It was a relief after all the sleeping bags and bunks and railroad earth. It was another of the many opportunities she's given me all her life to just stay home and write.[27]

My life has been blessed with similar rooms and kin, although my kin number beyond five to Barbara, and Leslie, and Kirsten, and

27. Kerouac, *Lonesome Traveler*, p. 104.

Spooky, and a couple more people I love who know and love me. Right now I live with my sister. I am living in the small bedroom she gave me to write in this summer. The bedroom is wonderful for writing. It has clean linen and a good wooden desk and four huge windows that open up onto a willow tree so that I am outside/inside all the time and the tree is part of daily life. I have learned to love this tree. It dances its daily grief all day and night for me, sending offerings of leaves onto my keyboard and reminding me that there is something else outside there. I'm looking out the window, and I'm looking at you.

Barbara lives only a few blocks away. Also close are Ad Infinitum and the playwright Forrest Gump. They are like brothers to me. I see all these people here, as I write this. They all know me. I do not need to tell them who I am because they already know. I do not have to give any accounts if I don't want to. They allow me to be silent or to talk long into the evening, and they do so with a grace and simplicity. My family is close by. When I saw them last week they gave me a golden aquamarine cross with the Virgin Mary as a gift. We talked about whether or not the couple whose old house I was moving into were asking a reasonable price for their washing machine. We talked about everyday things. I told my mother that I was dedicating my new book, *Representative Women*, to her, because she was my "Marmee." She said, "Thank you." This was so much more than any single e-mail exchange I ever had during that other time. But those twisted stares I had to climb seemed to meet me, seemed to be mine. Ever Yours. Ever Thine. Did I want a valentine?

MEANINGLESS EXCHANGES OF NON-WORDS
INTERRUPT THE NOT

Date: Tues., 11 Apr. 1995 18:50:17 EDT
To: "Dr. Rocket" <S.Paige.Baty@williams.edu>
From: A. Post Trophy
Subject: 3rd

1. how is Marylin fit into a hagiography, as does the widow or the spinster challenging the established order?

2. You should, if you ask me, establish a presence of some sort on line ecce pomo at least should get it's own pa(i)ge.

This is typical of the e-mail messages I received. Now most of my messages go unretrieved. Now I am more interested in *real* life exchanges. I do not care too much about establishing a presence on line. Now I like to see living people. Last night when we went out we met a guy who makes computer robots and his girlfriend is an artist from New York who draws comics. I told them about *e-mail trouble*. She was interested, and asked how bad it was for me. "Were you hooked? Are you talking three or four messages a day?" she asked me. I threw back my head and laughed and laughed and she was surprised. "No," I told this nice woman. "I was sunk. I'm talking up to thirty a day." She could hardly believe me. "Did you know these people?" "Some of them," I said, "but mostly not. Our relationships crashed on line." She was taken aback, as would make sense for anyone who lived in the real world of human beings. The talk drifted another way and I went into the bathroom at that right, good spot where the whole bathroom is slate and they have chalk and you get to write what you want on the walls. The last time I had been there I had posted a chalk note on the door, and I wanted to see if it was still there and what people had written back. I had written, "In the midst of the winter, I found in myself an invincible summer." I had signed it: Camus.

Women had written back to Camus. They wrote that the only true thing in life was love, and that they wanted it. They either had it or didn't, and so spake they on the chalkboard of a door at the bar where the door swings both ways at once and the bartender is really nice to you no matter what you ask for. There was a man/woman at the counter who had a pack of stick-on stars that s/he was using to decorate the blank white match books they gave to the patrons. Each one s/he made was different. S/he had been working on this project for hours. Every matchbook s/he made had handwriting on it, and a personal message, plus the number of the bar. The bartender was enjoying the scene, and gave me my own matchbook with the explanation, "We used to just be blank slates but now Diana makes these up for us so we have a personality too." I accepted Diana's matchbook with grace and sat back down. There are many ways of writing and more ways of making it home. These were the things I was beginning to remember, and I had to come home to do it.

STEP NINE:
Make direct amends to all persons you have harmed.

One time Albert Camus wrote a letter to me. He wrote it on February 15, 1953. I was not yet alive. It is entitled simply "Letter to P.B." When I read it I thought I had written it. When he wrote it, I believe he meant it. I reproduce it in part for you now to show you how it is for me:

My dear friend,

   I will begin with the apology I owe you for last Friday. . . . the question is what you describe as the difficulties of our relationship. On this point, what I have to say can be expressed simply: if you knew one quarter of my life and its obligations, you wouldn't have written a single line of your letter. But you cannot know them, and I neither can nor should explain them to you. The "haughty solitude" that you, along with many others who lack your quality, complain of, would be a blessing for me, if it existed. . . . The truth is that I fight time and other people for each hour of my work, usually without winning. I'm not complaining. My life is what I have made it, and I am the first person responsible for the way and the pace at which I spend it. . . . To be equal to everything today, I would need three lives and several hearts. Of the latter, I have only one, which can be judged, as I often judge it myself, to be of only average quality. . . . Each letter brings three others, each person ten, each book a hundred letters and twenty correspon- dents, while life continues, there is work to do, people I love and people who need me. Life continues, and some mornings, weary of the noise, discouraged by the prospect of the interminable work to keep after, sickened also by the madness of the world that leaps at you from the newspaper, finally convinced that I will not be equal to it and that I will disappoint everyone—all I want to do is sit down and wait for evening. This is what I feel like, and sometimes I yield to it. . . .

   Forgive me, in any case, for having disappointed you, and believe me to be,

Faithfully,
Albert Camus[28]

28. Albert Camus, *Lyrical and Critical Essays*, ed. Philip Thody, trans. Ellen Conroy Kennedy (New York: Knopf, 1968), pp. 342–344.

Albert Camus and letters. Letters often signify disappointment. E-mail seems at first to take care of that mess, but it can never take the place of any true correspondence. Antoine de Saint-Exupéry would never have written "Letter to a Hostage" on e-mail. Real letters mean really being there for the person to whom you are writing. But for the writer this is sometimes a difficult thing. There is so much work to be done, and a great deal of that is writing. Louisa May Alcott referred to her books as "letters." Perhaps writers are writing love letters to the world, and it is for this reason that they become lost. They try to negotiate an invisible world and their real relations, and they often make a mess of it. They end up feeling that they have disappointed everyone, including themselves. They look outside themselves for forgiveness, but they turn inside themselves to write. They sometimes sit all day and wait for the evening to come.

Date: Thurs., 02 Feb. 1995 11:09:16 EST
To: S.Paige.Baty@williams.edu
From: Juan Valdez
Subject: ive got a sentimental nostalgia for a place I never was.

When I got into e-mail trouble I suffered from nostalgia. I lived at a virtual site—Williams.edu—next door to a simulated frat on campus. There were nine big boys living there loudly, and they often had parties that spilled out onto the lawn and lasted way past dawn. Their dreams and conversations disrupted my sleep with a repetitive intensity. I was mesmerized and felt I needed to move away. Now I look back, and I see why. I had already gone to a college and had hung out at real frats. What was at first charming as a memory of a past youth ended in a nightmare of a morning where a young person came crashing through a window after screaming to all these people about how terrible his life was.

I was awakened by the scene, and ran out in my robe with the initials SPB my sister LTB gave to me for Christmas. It is my only item of clothing with my initials on it. She said she had it customized so I wouldn't give it away to someone else. I was always giving myself away. I will never forget the carnage of that day. I knew I had to move away. Liberal arts education was not all that it was cracked up to be, and now around me I saw the cracks it was making in the people that I loved. They were all giving up in one way or another. For them the school had been father and mother, and when they turned on it, or it on them, they did terrifying things to themselves and other people. Maybe it was the combination of a small face-to-face community and hyper-simulation. All I know is that a lot of them crashed, and they are still in the process of remaking themselves. Despite all the trouble, a part of me remains hopeful. Perhaps I am a melodramatic fool. Then again, I've spent my life in school.

```
Date:     Wed, 05 Apr. 1995 14:53:10 EDT
To:       "Dr. Rocket" <S.Paige.Baty@williams.edu>
From:     rusty
Subject:  Re:
```

i am not smart, remember.

I am also just getting your answering machine messages today.

Keep the gloves on.

In my efforts to escape I have lost all interest in schoolwork and begun to read manuals on computer languages in depth.

I hope you find equally stimulating time-savers.

Yours in oddity,

One Valdez

Number One was a student distancing herself from the enterprise of our small liberal arts college. She could not row with the crew anymore. I understand why. Some boundaries are a good thing. For a while, there, all boundaries were gone. I wanted more boundaries, and I have made them for myself. I set about making a home that feels like a home. But the time I'm telling you about was a time of no rooting, just occasional vases of flowers I'd put out for dinner parties. Everything was a big writing game, and if people came over they had to play. We mostly played that surrealist game, "The Exquisite Corpse." It's an add-on game. I don't want to play that game anymore, but some of the writing that came out of it was good. Nonetheless, I am happy now to be out of that scene. Things there got really mean. Everyone became a screen, and the Internet had a lot to do with it.

Date: 12/13/95
From: 4-Warned

The unsaid part of what you're thinking.
Finger me again for a different message.

Finger me and I will tell you that after the Fall I was in the students' classroom. They had evolved over my leave, if we want to be Darwinian about it. They were now "on line." Their first requests involved e-mail: could they reach me this way? They all used it to talk to each other. Other teachers were doing it. It seemed to open up possibilities of further connection, while insuring some privacy. Unlike the telephone, the e-mail system would allow me to reach them, or they me, at any hour of the day or night. I could choose when to reply: my dinners would go on uninterrupted by requests for paper extensions. Now there was a new system of extension, and this would allow access without intrusion. All that I needed to do was to give them my address, which I did, and they could write to me. It seemed a good idea at the time. I had no idea what I was in for. Like the flesh-eating virus, these correspondences consumed my body and life. I had less privacy in my life than any time I have ever known. People could contact me at two in the morning. I was awash in correspondence, yet I was alone.

C.—THE BODY OF THE LETTER.

LESSON I.

THE SALUTATION.

I. The *body* of the letter contains what you say to the person to whom you write.

As you would not enter another's room without rapping at the door, or begin a conversation with him without speaking his name, or in some polite way calling his attention, so you should not begin what you have to say to the person to whom you write without some form of greeting; as,

Sir:—　My dear Sir,—　Dear Friend,—
Gentlemen:—　My dear Mother:—

II. The greeting is called the *salutation*, and is the first thing in the body of the letter . . .[29]

Salutations, reader. I hope that this season finds you well. I hope that you have people with whom you correspond. I hope that you enjoyed something in your life today. I hope that you find some small happiness; or even better, some wild life. I am writing you: a letter. I do not know you. This is a story and I am writing you. Did I mention that I am called Paige Baty? How shall I call you? Can we have a conversation? What would it mean to talk to you? I am trying to learn to be a better listener. I am trying to stay, still.

Maybe it's not the author, but the reader, who is dead in our era. Maybe this is why I turned to e-mail for correspondents: dead readers, not dead letters. Invisible fingers pressing keys outside of the world I lived in. Mute voices sending me messages over time. So be gentle, virtual reader, and patient with the telling of the tale. You don't have to be here. Do you know where you are? What is the place you call home?

29. Mrs. N. L. Knox-Heath, *Elementary Lessons in English for Home and School Use, Part First: How to Speak and Write Correctly,* Teacher's Ed. (Boston: Ginn and Co., 1889), p. 232.

It was precisely about nothing, not being present. Not being there was what it was all about when you became a virtual correspondent. E-mail! The thrills of instantaneous correspondence. Democracy suddenly seemed a possibility. American vistas opened to me: suddenly I could correspond with anyone. I was excited by these correspondences, but as I look back today it appears to have taken place fifteen minutes ago, because such was the nature of these conversations and my conversion. Not all of those exchanges equaled a single second of face-to-face conversation and instruction I've had with people in my life. When I had real-time conversations I usually left imprinted by the very body of the person I was talking to. This was not true of the friends in my e-mail world. They were ephemeral. I thought that they taught me what it was to be in the moment again. I thought that they brought me back to childhood games after spending so much time with death. With a new kind of terminal fate screening my callers I set about making exchanges of meaning. I wrote the way I thought; I never edited myself.

Date: Tues., 28 Feb. 1995 09:28:58 EST
To: S.Paige.Baty@williams.edu
From: Jose.N.Marquez
Subject: 0

its raining outside, this heartless land
cleft valley, colored hills, barren hand

yet, you, your eyes will open brilliance
first conscious breath sucks in the grays
exhaling gold frost, diadems quicksilver

today it is sunny if torn from brute sky
warm, hot, if we teach our bodies to lie

your hand, fanned deck of cards in sleep
reaches through pane to lift the shutter

on the missing day, not there for those
rising yet again in yesterday's clothes
they unknowing the holy name of morning

you have slept through death and dreams
poisoned ears, fire burned out the eyes

yet realizing it as another's nightmare
shed tangled sheets and dangling bodies

came to the light of the secret sunrise
and witnessed the halos break from bark
the holy veins glowing faintly branches
holiest of hollies jutting out of roots

this dawning is yours alone sarah paige
only you would be born, reborn this day
is everlasting, and this two shall pass
and be one, be one, be one who is alive

be one who is alive and be free you are
you are, you are, this sarah paige baty

who lives and breathes in the spirit of
life glorious, in memoriam, everlasting

(The couple over the wall are fighting again. The little boy wants to know what time it is. "Six o'clock," his father yells. The boy asks again. "Tell me when it is six o'clock," he screams. "It's six o'clock," the father yells back. The mother is in the house, and she is angry. She cannot operate the VCR. "I don't know which button to push," she cries. The man is annoyed. "The one on the upper right." "I don't see it," she yells. They both start screaming at once: who are they yelling at? "Hurry up, hurry up, hurry up, hurry up." I have never seen these people, but I spend a lot of my days listening to their arguments. I want some resolution, but I never get it. They just scream this stuff out and sometimes I write it down. When the screaming gets too loud I put on my "Walkman" and play a game, "The Next Song Is Your Future with . . . " There is a loud, crashing noise coming from their yard. They are all yelling at once. "Get over here." There are many ways of disconnection in this world. The mother is screaming to the little boy, "Get out of the tent: RIGHT NOW.") The ghost voices of people haunt me. I try to use technology to block them out. I began to hear more voices, but they spoke in silent letters.

CUT TO THE INSTITUTION

First the students began to write me. Then I began to receive mail from other professors. My friends across the country found out I was using e-mail, and they too wrote. Then my friends in the UK and other countries found a cheaper way to communicate: e-mail me from work. When I went out to give a lecture people asked me for an e-mail address: after one lecture I received nine letters. The letters began to pile up but for the most part I wrote back.

Date: Wed, 15 Feb. 1995 06:38:40 EST
To: S.Paige.Baty@williams.edu
From: The Quick and The Dead
Subject: so you

all really think I should write more clear passages
so I guess I need to write more clear passages
and more clear passages, too. So now I think I will
try to write more clear passages. Ah, but in what
voice, and what will I say that hasn't already been
said a million times before.
So now I think I will try to write more clear passages.
pasajes. travel tickets in spanish.

Clear passages and travel tickets to virtual places. I saw sides of people I believed I wouldn't have seen if we had to meet in person. I discovered, momentarily, the hidden poetry of old friendships. In the beginning was the word, and the word was good. People took risks that I didn't think they'd take with me in person. They developed personas. These personas spoke to me in fragmented tones and terms. Now, it was not always so grand. Often the messages were trivial pursuits, asking only for a meeting or a book reference or a letter of recommendation. But often they were so much more . . . what appeared to be the stuff of the intimate. Some of this may be the result of where and when they were written: in students' rooms at two in the morning while they were working on a project. But in other cases I had real exchanges of meaning going.

I had a correspondence on the net with an old friend. I do not think it was e-mail that killed our friendship for a time, but it may have contributed to what seemed at the time a grand finale. What I thought was my last message from him was an e-mail telling me that he could no longer talk to me. When I received it I felt dead and cold inside. All of the intimacy was gone: our relationship was textual history. I returned to the graveyard.

I offer him this poem.

Widow's Weeds July 8, 1995

My poem now a subject needs
I'm writing in some widow's weeds
Sheltered from the neighbor's stare
Feeling sunlight on my hair
In a garden I now sit
East of Eden, out of it
Can this be a garden called?
There is a rose bush, after all.
To my left a lemon tree
broken pavement under me
But the yard is naught but weeds
Though the dirt here holds the seeds
of some garden that has passed
Even flowers do not last
A dry fountain sits amid
tufts of grass light brown, unbid
dandelions fill the square
nature's statutes of despair
Can I speak this space alive
shall I toil, sweat and strive?
I could put on canvas gloves
and pull the weeds up out of love
what then—plant seeds in their stead
corn or trees or flower beds?
Alas, the work would take so long
And the weeds out here are strong
They'd pull back if I approached
They'd spring up if I encroached
Now the sun is setting down
Darkened shadows cast the town
In the dark I mourn alone
In the garden, I lie prone
You are not forgotten, sun
Your glory shone in days now done.

Mourning overwhelmed me and became electric. I was surrounded by images of loss. I turned to the terminal as a place to stay connected and invisible. All of my live friends were passing away, and so I, too, passed the way of a hard-driven memory.

Maybe the show was called *The Fugitive*. Maybe the show was called *Car 54, Where Are You?* Maybe the show was called *Bonanza*. Maybe the show was *The Price Is Right*. Maybe it was *Guiding Light*. I searched for some beacon of hope, beckoning to me from the waters or island or wherever it was that I was lost. I could follow the beacon home to a safe harbor. I could finally be asleep and at peace. I thought about Lawrence's story "The Man Who Loved Islands." I thought about John Donne. I thought and fought but I never won the battle. I could not get a good night's sleep. Insomnia has always been my curse. I sleep very little, and then not well. At this time I gave up sleeping almost altogether. I needed ways to fill my time. Now this seems strange, but at the time I had hours to kill. Killing time is what the Internet is about: inertia and the spectacle of connection. Why not send out dead letters all day and night? Entropy set in, and the computer gave me a tool to turn the stuff of entropy into writing. Writing nothing from ground zero: I was just counting sheep. There are better ways to get to sleep. My friends tried to remind me that I was caught in a script, and that real dreaming would be a better solution to my problem. Then I did not listen well. Now I do. Here was one such reminder, a remainder of days gone by. Those days appear to me as dreams gone by.

A FRIEND TRIES TO INTERVENE

Date: Mon., 09 Jan 1995 13:51:06 EST
To: Paige Baty <S.Paige.Baty@williams.edu
From: Tennessee Williams
Subject: Re: hi there

Paige, this Racer X is a kid. He's cute, he's a "man's man", he's smart. But, alas and alack(ey), he's a kid. Your lack should be under lock and key. If anyone can get in there, they'll be a keymaster to your paigemaker – you don't have to worry about keeping the lines open, keeping trouble at bay. Watch the tv, get the medicine, tune out the static coming from the tractor-trailer rig-by, find yourself a good computer (after all, adam can't be wrong - a good computer is better than the tree of knowledge), and let the cpu be you or just be yours or you could be its, but not if you name it something like, mr. machine, in which case it could be a mister to your ms.

I think therefore you are. Ha - that's a little joke Schlegel told me, but it reminds me of something we talked about at 5:45 this morning. See, just because you think it - doesn't mean it is.

Be wary of substitutions - that's not thinking just slipping (from a to be on down to z - remember _To the Lighthouse_ and the folly of barking up that alphabetical tree). These things all flow together, really bleed together, when the vessels have leaks and the ship seems to be sinking.

You on the other hand, are a Titan - not the Titanic. You can walk on water. Remember that people are 75% water. OK, that's my $.02 - hope all is going better.

DON'T REPEAT YOURSELF - i.e., don't obsess.

STEP TEN:
Continue to take personal inventory and promptly admit when you are wrong.

Termination of reminder, but not of repetition. The Internet was taking over. We were all caught in the same game. It seemed fun for a while, but later it got hard to quit. Once you are hooked it is not easy to give things up. You find yourself checking your e-mail compulsively, as if some great message is waiting for you. The medium becomes the message. You no longer know why you are doing it, but it becomes a force of habit. It is a hard habit to kick. When a hyper-reality replaces your daily life where do you go for comfort, assurance, a point of deterrence—Disneyland? My friends occupied the same state of simulation I had come to know and try and forget. For some of them it was just e-mail; for others virtual experiences. One friend wrote to me of his first experience with "lived" virtual reality:

```
Date:      Fri., 03 Feb. 1995 12:51:37 PST
To:        "Dr. Rocket" <S.Paige.Baty@williams.edu>
From:      Ad Hominum
Subject:   Welcome to Reality(tm)
```

I went and experienced the new MagicEdge(tm). It is a flight simulator place that lets you fly fighter planes in a virtual world with 5 other people.

The emphasis is on Reality and the Real, and how more Real their Reality is than the competition's.

When they first boot up they greet you with: Welcome to Reality

The software was developed by a company in Dallas called Paradigm Systems. The database for the world is known as the Vampire database. Vamping the Real.

The scenario is drug interdiction. You are briefed by a young kid in a jumpsuit on how there are enemies trying to run drugs across the border of your imaginary country. Your goal is to intercept these bad guys, and blow them up.

I couldn't make up something weirder if I tried.

I have s(c)ene our future, rendered (like a piece of meat) in 3D, and everything has already been trademarked. [big sigh]

He had seen the future and it was murder. It was all done in the name of entertainment. The wired and the weird were morphing, while the system kept evolving. All the borders were dissolving.

I opened the July 1995 issue of *Wired* and found an advertisement for Envoy Wireless Communication. The ad featured a crazed man wearing his Envoy head gear (called the Magic Cap). The Magic Cap allows the wearer to "send text and handwritten messages via radio, phone/fax or infrared." The Magic Cap will organize its wearer's days: The ad advised, "Let 'smart agents' automatically reschedule meetings, update addresses, etc., while you get on with business." This business called living. Mike Backe, the man in the ad, gives the following testimony:

With Envoy I don't get "stuck" in meetings. I send and receive

messages, right at the conference table. No post-meeting back-
logs. Envoy levels out my workload. I love it! . . . Envoy thinks
like I do. Sounds weird, but while I'm physically at one meeting,
I'm part of three or four others going on in my Envoy. I'm
E-mailing, I'm faxing, I'm wireless, man!

Wireless man. A civilization coming unglued as it gets on line. Talking to everyone at once, through the magic cap. The magic cap is a sort of cyber-secretary, fixing the life of its wearers. Maybe there will be a new Envoy sit-com, and instead of Major Nelson discovering Jeannie, Darren will buy an Envoy after Sam has been burnt at the stake and find that his magic cap will work better for him than his witch-of-a-wife and her meddling relatives. Dreams of witches and genies and magic caps are the stuff of fairy tales, and now such is the material of our technology. Amazing, what technology can do. Press: Save humanity. Everybody's on line and wireless, talking incessantly to others even while sitting alone or at board meetings. I don't want anyone to have that much access to my brain: car phones and answering machines are bad enough. I'll wait till they patent the magic cloak that makes me invisible. Hit Delete key.

The matrix was erasing me even as I came to, in a simulated experience of my life. Maybe I should have just dialed 911, or just watched *Rescue 911*. Where was I? Beam me up, Scotty. Who is scripting this show?

The terminal site consumed my being. Things began to get scary.

I was caught in the web of the computer's artificial life. My friends, too, were caught in the web. It was like a real-life experience of the "Alien" series: we were surrounded by the matrix of death that fed on human flesh. We were addicts. Many of the people I corresponded with at this time checked their e-mail compulsively. What message were they hoping to get? Were they waiting for the word to become flesh? Would it? Maybe God would send one of us an e-mail, or some demi-god. We waited for the word, but the word began to mean less and less. Just as the flesh-eating virus was killing people in Zaire, I found that many of my closest friends had been consumed by the e-mail virus: they had caught the computer bug.

We were being eaten alive. It was all text, subtext, confessions peeling away layers of skin which so often cover polite conversation. I wanted a more perfect union with my old friends and my new-found friends, but we lost context. I could contact them at almost any site, but we were less and less together. I learned the meaning of solitude. Solitude and information went hand in hand. They both followed the width of a band, stretching across an America on line and off track, lots of people looking back. I write as I hack. I write as I lack.

Date: Thurs., 12 Jan 1995 13:58:23 EST
To: S.Paige.Baty@williams.edu
From: don caballero
Subject: if you order the stamps now...

1. Frank Sinatra gave Marilyn a pet poodle which she named Maf... short for "Mafia."

2. The real FBI file on Marilyn has never surfaced.

3. Joe DiMaggio sent red roses to Marilyn's grave three times a week after her death.

4. Marilyn was paid $4 an hour for her first modeling assignment.

5. Marilyn's dress was actually sewn around her just before she sang her famous Happy Birthday song to President Kennedy at Madison Square Garden in New York City.

Taken from the pocket guide 99 Little Known Facts About Marilyn Monroe--yours free, when you order these stamps.

by the way you can order the stamps by www @ http://www.kiosk.net/marilyn

see ya

It was all one big home-shopping club and I had become a client. I did not like what I found in the bargain basement of ideas. I did not want to buy what it had to sell. I lost the sense of touch and smell. I lost my body in the mail. I found my fingers hitting keys.

I surfed the Web but its waves drowned me. If e-mail teaches you one thing it is that you are alone. You write alone. You see your friends alone, on a screen. You read their words alone; in a room of your own. Sure, I agree with Virginia Woolf, but this was taking it too damn far. Now, some kinds of solitude are good for the soul, but not this one in particular. This was soul-murder, or a life of misplaced dreams.

CUT/PASTE/LOVE'S BODY

Unborn—in the womb, then; asleep; and dreaming. Withdrawn from the environment, or split from the environment; as in schizophrenia. As Blake saw, there is a fission, a duplication, a division. Withdrawn into a cave (or womb) which is himself; as Blake would say, the Self-hood. The womb into which the sleeper withdraws is at the same time his own body. The dreamer sinks into himself. And makes himself a whole new world; a man-made world, in the deepest sense. A whole new world out of the body of the dreamer, a world which is his cave.[30]

Solitude and love and the womb. I saw them all come together at that time. I withdrew into a cave of myself: I caved in. I sank. I made the world over as myself and my personas. I made a body of a matrix not of flesh and blood but silicon and circuit. The world became the dream, instead of the cave. I needed to get out in the light and see that it was all a shadow-play, but the matrix was comforting, even as it suffocated me. I curled up in a fetal position and wrote myself away, gave myself away, to invisible correspondents. We were all chained together on that same damn seat, looking at the same shadows on the wall, but we dreamed it was real. And I want to stress this: it appeared to be real. Maybe because it was a man-made body, not a body of woman born.

It was the artificial matrix. It was the dominatrix of relationships; it was the male man invested in corporations of being. These are named Apple, and Silicon Graphics and IBM and Hewlett Packard and such are they named, and it is not for nothing that the first name is apple. The dangerous knowledge of this form of reproduc-

30. Brown, *Love's Body*, p. 49.

tion/production was taking place in an Astroturf Eden.

It came from men sitting in solitude dreaming of a world man made, made of man. They were making this world and we came to live in it. It was worse for the women, but bad for all. We were building a tower of Babel, and we were in for a fall. We thought it was fun when we were doing it, but we were destroying ourselves.

```
Date:     Wed, 15 Mar 1995 11:31:36 CST
To:       S.Paige.Baty@williams.edu
From:     Henny Young, Man
Subject:  Why the chicken crossed the road...
```

Hey Paige,

hi. This bit of silliness showed up in my mailbox. Some of it's pretty bad, but a couple struck me as worth reading. Of course, I leave it to you to decide which ones fall into which categories (hopefully, you'll assign at least some to the humorous side).

> >> So why did the chicken cross the road?
> >>
> >> Plato: For the greater good.
> >>
> >> Karl Marx: It was a historical inevitability.
> >>
> >> Machiavelli: So that its subjects will view it with admiration,
> >> as a chicken which has the daring and courage to boldly cross
> >> the road, but also with fear, for who among them has the
> >> strength to contend with such a paragon of avian virtue? In
> >> such a manner the princely chicken's dominion is maintained.
> >>
> >> Jacques Derrida: Any number of contending discourses may be
> >> discovered within the act of the chicken crossing the road,
> >> and each interpretation is equally valid as the authorial intent
> >> can never be discerned, because structuralism is DEAD,
> >> DAMMIT, DEAD!
> >>
> >> Timothy Leary: Because that's the only kind of trip the
> >> Establishment would let it take.
> >>
> >> Douglas Adams: Forty-two.
> >>
> >> Nietzsche: Because if you gaze too long across the Road, the
> >> Road gazes also across you.
> >>
> >> Jean-Paul Sartre: In order to act in good faith and be true to
> >> itself, the chicken found it necessary to cross the road.
> >>

> >> Ludwig Wittgenstein: The possibility of "crossing" was
> >> encoded into the objects "chicken" and "road", and
> >> circumstances came into being which caused the actualization
> >> of this potential occurrence.
> >>
> >> Albert Einstein: Whether the chicken crossed the road or the
> >> road crossed the chicken depends upon your frame of
> >> reference.
> >>
> >> Aristotle: To actualize its potential.
> >>
> >> Buddha: If you meet the chicken on the road, kill it.
> >>
> >> Howard Cosell: It may very well have been one of the most
> >> astonishing events to grace the annals of history. An historic,
> >> unprecedented avian biped with the temerity to attempt such
> >> an Herculean achievement formerly relegated to Homo sapien
> >> pedestrians is truly a remarkable occurrence.
> >>
> >> Salvador Dali: The Fish.
> >>
> >> Emily Dickinson: Because it could not stop for death.
> >>
> >> Ralph Waldo Emerson: It didn't cross the road; it transcended
> it.
> >>
> >> Ernest Hemingway: To die. In the rain.
> >>
> >> The Sphinx: You tell me.

Everything was an in(ternet) joke only I wasn't sure how funny it
was anymore. Bits and bytes of information like this crossed my path
like chickens every day. What came first, the chicken or the megs? I
liked being party to cultural parodies that swept across populations
like a virus, but I also began to feel weakened by the same. So much
of the same. I could recognize the codes and the jokes and the names
but they were not for me, about me: I was just another anonymous
body logged onto some site where somebody's listserver would spit
out a bit of nonsense or poetry or humor or advice and I could take
it in alone. Of course I could always forward the mail to more people, but I had begun to feel chained to the letter of e-mail, like a bad
chain letter one receives in junior high school that tells of the horrors
that will befall all those who do not comply to its demands. I was
hooked on a circuit of communication that seemed never-ending.
There were some good moments on the way, but my writing and

my life suffered. I spent hours that I could have spent with a friend or a book or writing a book, writing to other people.

When I decided to write *e-mail trouble* I asked my friends for my old correspondence. Everyone I asked had already deleted my messages and so these purloined letters disappeared into the matrix dead as a still-born child I was never to know, name, embrace. All those words had been erased. My tissues bled out of me this time.

I felt like one of the senders of dead letters in Melville's *Bartleby the Scrivener*. All my messages of life had been sent to death. Someone just had to hit a delete key and they were gone. Why, you might ask, didn't I have them, why couldn't I save them? My computer had contracted several viruses and the whole hard drive had to be replaced. I lost a lot when my memory crashed, and that included all the e-mail I'd sent those I knew. Much of what I lost was poetry. The rest of what I lost goes beyond words. I had believed in communication, birth, and connection. I had saved everyone else's e-mail. Now I found that I had been deleted. I had not been saved in someone else's artificial memory. The part of me that had written was dead.

I felt a profound loss at the death of my letters. They had been my attempts to reach out to others and they no longer existed. Of course this happens with most texts; I just didn't expect it to happen so quickly with my virtual community. The virtual Paige was dead. She had an artificial memory that had crashed. Memory with no past. What was going on? I was losing myself. There are other ways of remembering. Computers and corporations do not hold the patent on memory: they sell a three-penny soap opera cure. They give you this world and it's a game and in it you make up your name. What I miscarried will remain forever without a name, but I have felt its pain.

NOTES FROM UNDERGROUND

I have spent years trying to solve the riddle of Bartleby the Scrivener. I lived with Bartleby for a time in the Midwest. As our imitation of life continued it seems that he answered me so often with the words

STEP FIVE: Admit to God, yourself, and another human being your wrongs.

"I would prefer not to." We stopped talking. Our last form of correspondence was e-mail. There were times before when things were different: he was my audience, and I was his. Now, it seems, things were over. I could not take this ending, and wanted to rewrite the story. I wanted for the two of us to correspond again. I begged Bartleby to talk to me, to meet me in a place of mutual exchange. Maybe the postage system could save us, or possibly the answering machine. I made calls; I wrote letters. I tried to find a way to right the past. But what is one to do when corresponding with Bartleby? He will not talk or listen. There are rumors as to why he is the way he is, and I reproduce one of them for you now.

The report was this: that Bartleby had been a subordinate clerk in the Dead Letter Office at Washington, from which he had been suddenly removed by a change in the administration. When I think over this rumour, hardly can I express the emotions which seize me. Dead letters! Does it not sound like dead men? Conceive a man by nature and misfortune prone to a pallid hopelessness, can any business seem more fitted to heighten it than that of continually handling these dead letters, and assorting them for the flames? For by the cartload they are annually burned. Sometimes from out the folded paper the pale clerk takes a ring—the finger it was meant for, perhaps, moulders in the grave; a banknote sent in swiftest charity—he whom it would relieve, nor eats nor hungers any more; pardon for those who died despairing; hope for those who died unhoping; good tidings for those who died stifled by unrelieved calamities. On errands of life, these letters speed to death.

Ah, Bartleby! Ah, humanity![31]

31. Herman Melville, "Bartleby the Scrivener," in *The Writings of Herman Melville*, vol. 9 (Evanston and Chicago: Northwestern University Press and The Newberry Library, 1987), p. 45.

Bartleby, my Bartleby, is hard to forget. I am stuck on someone who is stuck on dead letters. The lack of correspondence inflects Bartleby's life. I am a failed correspondent. I take some faith in time, and that the passing of time will change the present. For the record, it takes two for any correspondence to succeed or fail. And when you let a third party into this formulation things become very messy.

You are dealing with invisible populations of relation. I know that Bartleby will not always be Bartleby: we all change our handles. Maybe I am waiting for the day when Bartleby becomes Emerson, or perhaps Candide. He will write his own stories, and send his own letters. He will love life again. Bartleby will no longer be married to mourning. Bartleby will let go of the things that make him withdraw from the world. I still have some simple faith. I do not believe that Bartleby is permanently gone: I prefer to think of him as sleeping— though not with counsellors and kings. The sleep I imagine is the sort from which one can wake up and begin again. Correspondence would become again a possibility, as we would leave the matrix and enter into the world.

Sleepers, awake. Sleep is separateness; the cave of solitude is the cave of dreams, the cave of the passive spectator. To be awake is to participate, carnally and not in fantasy, in the feast; the great communion.[32]

Date: Wed, 28 Aug 1996 16:41:11 EDT
To: Williams-Faculty@williams.edu, Williams-
             Staff@williams.edu
From: Perry.O.Hanson@williams.edu
Subject: August Virus Attack
Return-Path: @williams.edu

August 28, 1996
Dear Williams Faculty and Staff,

The August Virus Attack created a huge disaster for the Williams
community. The nature of the Jerusalem D Virus (a new variant
according
to Novell) created a particularly challenging task for recovery. The
lack of
a disaster recovery plan for such situations forced us into ad hoc
solutions.
e-mail reports during the last weeks provided details about
the problems that were faced in resolving the damage created
by the Virus so I shall focus on where we go from here.

The Jerusalem D Virus launched itself on 4 August; it began
corrupting
tables that describe file organization and overwriting data files.
Not until
10 August did we find the Virus, and the Virus creator's phrase,

32. Brown, *Love's Body*, p. 255.

"Nyah,
nyah, got ya, you're [expletive deleted]." It took some time to discover
that the virus attacked the lowest level of the disk structure; in the end we
literally had to replace the physical disks. Our data recovery firm could not
recover any data on the corrupted disks.

For the next months I have set the following priorities so we can deal with
another disaster more deliberately. We shall put a disaster recovery plan in
place for our network services. (We have a formal disaster recovery plan
for the administrative systems.) The plan will most likely include locally
available systems and applications on microcomputers and a shared backup
strategy. We must have a tiered plan that supports the use of standalone,
basic applications on the desktop along with local backup and local printing
as well as access to network services. We must educate each other about
backup requirements, virus prevention, and firewalls.

To focus our attention on these issues, I have created a Desktop Systems
team to provide day-to-day support for microcomputers and to develop a
disaster recovery plan that includes locally available systems and
application software. We will work closely with you to develop these
services.

I look forward to working with you, and I will keep you informed in a
variety of ways about our progress.

Chief Technology Officer

Getting over the virus has been difficult. It seems to have been with me for years. Memory is caught up in this virus, and sometimes it is a path to recovery. The recovery process has been rocky, but there are places to turn for support. I have turned away from the technologies of williams.edu. I have gone back to the simple process of telling stories to remember who I am. The author, Gloria Watkins, who writes under the pseudonym "bell hooks," knows about naming and memory. In *Talking Back: Thinking Feminist, Thinking Black*, she reminds the reader of another way of naming:

To me naming is about empowerment. It is also a source of tremendous pleasure. I name everything—typewriters, cars, most things I use—that gives something to me. It is a way to acknowledge the life force in every object. Often the names I give to things and people are related to my past. They are a way to preserve and honor aspects of that past. Speaking of ancestor acknowledgment within African traditions has been a way to talk about how we learn from folks we may never have known but who live again in us. In Western traditions, this same process is talked about as the collective unconscious, the means by which we inherit the wisdom and ways of our ancestors. Talking with an elderly black man about names, he reminded me that in our southern black folk tradition we have the belief that a person never dies as long as their name is remembered, called. When the name bell hooks is called, the spirit of my great-grandmother rises.[33]

Bell hooks. bell hooks. bell hooks. Now the spirit of your great-grandmother has arisen to help me with my naming. I, too, name everything. I named my first bicycle "Mario." I named my bed "Excalibur." I named the imaginary ghost in my closet "the balloon man." I name the books I have not yet written. I named my imaginary daughter "Tuesday Grace." I named my friend "Ad Infinitum." And as I grew up I wrote my name again and again in every space I could find: Paige Baty/Paige Baty/Paige Baty. When I read my old journals I find pages filled with that name. Was I trying to speak myself into being, or calling on some dead ancestress? Was I trying to become real, to remember that I was there? When did I stop calling on Paige Baty? I can barely scrawl my signature now: all I can do is type. All I am is type. Type: FACE. I was trying to face up to myself. It was an act of contrition with the computer now mediating

33. bell hooks,
*Talking Back:
Thinking Feminist,
Thinking Black*
(Boston: South End
Press, 1989), p. 166.

between me and the source of infinity. What should I call that source: God, chaos, humanity, myself, Mary? Matrix? Dominatrix? Into which womb was I returning to be reborn?

```
Date:     Fri., 10 Feb, 1995 11:57:47 EST
To:       S.Paige Baty@williams.edu
From:     4-warned
Subject:  dinner

if you can fit me in
the crush
factor, independent study faction,
adviser to the world, fracture
l
ater
```

In that cold bloodless matrix I renamed myself. Repetition. I first became "Dr. Rocket." I then took on more personas, "Rosetta Stone" and "Paige Nation"; "Paige Maker" and "Spaige." My friends began to call me by these names. It was all getting very blurry. People I barely knew called me "Spaige." I felt it was a nickname that had to be earned: it was given to me by two students. It was my fake French theorist name. They named me for fun and play, and because we were friends. Now people I didn't know were calling me Spaige. I didn't like it. No one ever called me Doctor Rocket to my face. I asked my students to call me "Maestro." It stuck, but only like a Post-it Note. So much for my notions of grandeur. I use Paige Baty like a pseudonym anyway: who the hell is she? One in a series of people I invented as I went along.

```
Date:     Tues., 13 Dec. 1994 02:44:07 EST
To:       s.paige.baty@williams.edu
From:     junior varsity
Subject:  it's not often

that i introduce you to people
Also, here is the kid, maybe not *the*
kid, but a kid to whom I want to pass
on a torch, so to speak.
I think maybe he's definitely worth your
very close reading of the following exchange
between me and his COMPUTER program at
2:35 in the morning during Finals Week:
```

bigbird:
Login name: 97   In real life: Hrm?
Directory: /home/97   Shell: /usr/local/bin/bash
On since Dec 12 19:25:55 on ttyuf from student_97
6 hours 31 minutes Idle Time
New mail received Tues. Dec. 13 02:24:22 1994;
unread since Tues. Dec. 13 02:24:20 1994

Plan:
You've just fingered the kid.
It is 02:37, on Tues., Dec. 13, 1994.
You are #1 in the list of people who have fingered me since the
last time I logged out. Hold on while I think of something to say.
Thanks for fingering me, Number One.

Rule 46, Oxford Union Society, London:
Any member introducing a dog into the Society's premises shall
be liable to a fine of one pound. Any animal leading a blind
person shall be deemed to be a cat.

Finger me again for a different message.

bigbird:
Login name: In real life: Hrm?
Directory: /home/97   Shell: /usr/local/bin/bash
On since Dec. 12 19:25:55 on ttyuf from student_97
6 hours 32 minutes Idle Time
New mail received Tues. Dec. 13 02:24:22 1994;
unread since Tues. Dec. 13 02:24:20 1994

Plan:
You've just fingered the kid
It is 02:38, on Tues., Dec. 13, 1994.
You are #4 in the list of people who have fingered me since the
last time I logged out. Hold on while I think of something to say.
Thanks for fingering me, Number One.

The best book on programming for the layman is "Alice in
Wonderland"; but that's because it's the best book on anything for
the layman.

Finger me again for a different message.

So I met a new person through an introduction based on a relation a friend had with his computer. Was I meeting a person or a
program? In this case, I've come to know the person and have come
to ignore the program. But this was the exception, not the rule, in
relationships I began over the net. Most of those relationships crashed.

COMPUTER MOUSE TOO

And this, said the narrator of the story, is where the e-mail trouble really began. It all started with an innocent remark to a colleague who had just spoken on the phone with her friend in New Orleans. At that time, I loved the city of New Orleans, or thought that I did. It was the site of perpetual indulgence, the site of many great plantations and place where the gens de couleur had a separate system under American slavery. Tulane, one of its universities, housed one of the best collections in African American studies, and I was a lover of archives. It was a city below sea level where the dead were buried above ground. It was a city where you could buy a drink in a plastic cup and walk through the French Quarter breathing in the sultry night air—a drunken Disneyland for adults. It was the city where Anne Rice wrote about vampires and mummies and witches, generations of witches in the thrall of a male spirit called "Lasher." It housed the "garden district," a simulated real neighborhood of the Mayfair witch stories and intricate architecture. And around the city were the swamps, filled with alligators and fish and birds. I am losing myself in the city, and I need to go back to the office where the trouble began.

Where was I? In an office in the cold of a New England winter. I had been boxed up too long. When my colleague said that her friend was in New Orleans, I replied, "I'd love to go there again." Ten minutes later I received an e-mail invitation from a man I had never met asking me to join him and his friends for the Jazz Festival. It would be crowded, but should be lots of fun. And so, being an impulsive person, I said "yes."

Date: Sun, 26 Mar 1995 19:05:48 EST
To: s.paige.baty@williams.edu
From: The Good Man
Subject: My favorite, myself

Dear "S":

Thanks for the response. It does sort of sound like you think like
you might actually show up at this jazzfest thing.

> I, for one, feel like I think it will be fun
> attending someone else's big chill type of a weekend

I dunno. The big chill was so glamorous and everyone was so
successful in their own way--even the guy with no balls was
a supercool ball-less wonder.

We're just losers. Ever seen "Return of the Secaucus Seven"?
Kind of like that, minus the women, minus the sexual tension,
minus the intelligence, minus the political commitment, minus
even the goofy volleyball scene in which the recent-ex turns
up by picking up the out-of-bounds ball.

> and if you treat me as horribly as you have intimated then I'll
> just write about you later in some novel which will be a thinly
> veiled portrait of an attorney as a young or once young man

I didn't intimate that I would treat you horribly, did I? OK, maybe
I did. But if you think threatening me with literary infamy is a
disincentive, you've picked the wrong frustrated-writer-and-
former-literature-grad-student-turned-attorney to pick on. I'd
love to be in your novel.

> if you are going to be cruel and indifferent to
> me without ever meeting me then I think that I will just repeat
> lines to myself from Gone With The Wind and I will feel quite
> southern and grand and above it all and that will be that.

Which lines?

> but why don't you just be nice instead? It's generally a lot
> more fun, in the long run. trust me. I've been there.

Bad choice of words, that "nice". During our college days, we used
to look at nice as an expletive deletive. But you have my word:
if you do show up, I will be nice. I actually tend to be very nice
when I'm inebriated (I'm one of those gushy, sentimental type
drunks), and since I plan to be inebriated as much of the time
as possible (it's the only way I can think of to put up with my
friends), I might be almost bearable company. Although, be
warned, I have a disgusting sense of humor (which I tried to hint

at in my last letter), which is a trait shared by the whole crew that will be in attendance.

>> are you really that horrible?

Yes and no.

>> how do you live with yourself?

I don't. I actually live about two doors down.

So, maybe I'll see you in new orleans. Maybe I'll get another reply from you (since you answered my last e-mail, which Luther thought was kind of tasteless, even for me, this is possible). Thanks for the entertainment.

Yours Truly and all that,

The Goodman

I was intrigued by this faceless, bodiless voice. He seemed to me so full of life. He had a great wit. He was well-read. I was excited to meet him. We began to correspond on a regular basis. He sent me a *real* letter in the mail complete with a photo and poem. I felt like I'd joined a computer fating service. This should have been my first clue that I was in for a hard fall.

Date: Mon., 01 May 1995 16:23:24 EDT
To: S.Paige.Baty@williams.edu
From: The Other
Subject: New Orleans

Dear Paige:

Hey, you never let me know whether you got my letter. I never got anything from you, despite promises of poetry and the like. Oh well.
So, have things mellowed out for you at all? Make sure to leave all that heavy shit behind you if you can. It's party time. I mowed my lawn, which was beginning to look like some unexplored region of the Amazon. (Yup, being a homeowner makes one do goofy things like mow the lawn on a sunny sunday afternoon instead of inside watching hoops like any sane person would; although I did type up one memo that needed doing while watching the end of the Chicago-Charlotte game on sunday.)

I'm looking forward to finally meeting you in person rather than as a telephone voice. See you soon.

Affectionately (or whatever),

XXXX

I was still resolved that I was to make this trip, but as I began to find out more and more about the group I was filled with anxiety. They were an anxious lot, to be sure, especially my host. He wanted me to select menus in advance, and advised me on what to pack. He was a vegetarian, and hated smoking. He wrote me a letter about smoking in his house. I hadn't planned to, but when I received the letter I was offended. I showed it to several friends who also found it odd; but of course, they were my friends. What I didn't know, but should have guessed, was that he was forwarding my exchanges to his male friends who were also coming. E-mail trouble was just firing up. I had no idea what I was in for.

Confession one: i am that i am. I am an academic, but i prefer to think of myself as a thinker. I live in a strange world, but so do you, and we are strangers in the same strange land. This land is littered with waste: bodies, junk mail, newspapers, chewing gum wrappers, old memos, bottle tops, white noise, bandwidths of communication, AM radio songs, shoelaces, old books, Taco Bell commercials, flyers for any and everything. This is called detritus. We all experience it everyday. How much garbage do you, one person, generate or dispose of in a day? Think about it.

Try this challenge: for one week keep every extra bit of everything that comes your way. Save scraps. If you eat at home, don't wash the dishes. If you eat out, bring whatever is left over home and let it rot for awhile. Save your junk mail. Take every piece of paper someone on the streets hands to you. Keep your pizza boxes. Let the coke cans stack in your kitchen. Don't do your laundry. Live among the trash you accumulate.

Maybe then you'll remember the world before garbage disposals and septic tanks and drains and hidden sewer systems and trash compactors and dumps and garbage pickup and mail delivery every day and newspapers, newspapers, newspapers in your mail box; and of course, the inevitable bills. Parking tickets and tax notices and credit card bills and student loans and things you don't remember buying, but there are the costs being delivered unto you. Sure, maybe you get a thrill from the occasional Victoria's Secret catalogue, or by cruising through *Wired* or reading the *Times* or checking your stocks, but it's all part of the same problem, so get real to it, girl, and fess up. We are overwhelmed by garbage. How often in that garbage do you receive a personal, handwritten note from a correspondent, a loved one? How often do you send these notes?

We are so busy with this business called living that it is hard to sit down and write a real letter at the end of the day. E-mail, however, takes no time, no space, or place. Just plug in and jack off.

```
Date:     Fri., 28 Apr. 1995 19:52:45 EDT
To:       S.Paige.Baty@williams.edu
From:     The Good Man
Subject:  Re: Latest Odds
```

Dear Paige:

> **Affectionately The Good Man?**
> **Huh?**

Yes. I think I explained this in our phone conversation last P.M. as a good thing, meaning an attempt at acknowledging affection and fondness. Better look at Chapter 17 on guyspeak: "Sharing Our Feelings? Guys Don't Have Feelings, Only Muscles."

Affection is as affection does.

The Good Man

Affection or affectation or the flattering of affect? Real letters are written by hand. They take time to write. They imply a solitude of spirit which feels occasion to sit down, take time from a day, and send a letter. In the nineteenth century and early into this one, people would have correspondences for years—maybe forty or fifty years. After they died, if they were famous, maybe somebody collected them, or maybe they are scattered like dust at a dozen odd libraries. Still, I have read these letters. I had to get to know the character of the voice I was reading. When I read Louisa May Alcott's letters I felt like an archaeologist, digging among the ruin of verbs and nouns and names I didn't recognize to know her. I wanted her more and more. The letters made me desire her. They awakened in me a longing for a correspondent: Nietzsche's echo. Echoing and re-echoing. I read her journals, her sister's letters, her accounts. I began to recollect her. I felt I knew and loved her. Looking back on our relationship, her death may have had a lot to do with it. I was, after all, pouring over her private notes, and they were not addressed to me or even posterity. She wrote them to her family.

There are many relationships between persons deemed great or unknown that hinged upon the letter. I study these, and am particularly interested in nineteenth-century women and men of letters. I am also taken by accounts of relationships based upon letter writing: in addition to reading the letters themselves I scour the Berkshire hills for books filled with thoughts on women and letters. Most recently, at "Dog Ear's Books," I came upon the rather obscure, *What Can a Woman Do?* The subject is not what you think it to be—the author, Mrs. M. L. Rayne, is laying out possibilities for women in the business and literary world. These positions range from cook to photographer to colorer of photographs to teacher to nurse to government clerk. Yet Rayne waxes rhapsodic at moments in the text on the greatness and strength of women throughout history. I include for you here one of my favorite passages, from her chapter, "Friendship among Women."

What devotion could be more lasting and heroic than that of the Princess Lamballe for her unfortunate friend, Marie Antoinette? They had shared each other's confidences in the happy days of prosperity, and, when evil days came upon the queen, the princess could not be persuaded to seek her own safety by leaving the palace. When at last she was summoned to the bedside of a dying relative, Marie Antoinette sent her a letter begging her not to return. "Your heart," she wrote, "would be too deeply wounded; you would have too many tears to shed over my misfortunes, you who love me so tenderly. Adieu, my dear Lamballe; I am always thinking of you, and you know I never change!" But the princess hastened back to her imperiled friend, and through all those terrible last days of the sack, the pillage, and the prison, clung to her with a devotion as tender as it was heroic. When they strove to draw from her at the trial something prejudicial to the royal victim, when the mob which had lost semblance of humanity, with wild, red eyes, howled like wolves for blood, she preferred death to treachery, and her beautiful head, with its wealth of golden locks, in which was concealed this last letter from Marie Antoinette, was elevated on a pike before the prison window of the woman for whom she had died.[34]

Now here is a story of correspondence at great cost, and of great worth. Two women who are lifelong friends: they correspond. One implores the other, via letter, to "save herself." The friend does not have this sort of character, but rather must return to be with her friend during her trials. The cost: her life. The image of the Princess's head stuck on a pike outside Marie Antoinette's window is astounding. The prisoner must espy her beloved stuck as if on a pin: permanently silenced, yet adorned with tresses that boast the hand that wrote with another pen. This is one version of love, desire, and letters. That the letter remains there inside the head—or, rather, trapped in its golden locks—shows the power of their correspondence. Even with a warning letter the princess did not desert her friend. Marie Antoinette, while unlucky herself if we think of her ending, was blessed with a true correspondent: her friend was willing to put her head under the blade rather than speak out against her. The letter must have been her greatest keepsake: it kept her going. The letter she secreted on her body before she was to die. The letter that stood in for her great friend, the queen. I wonder who found the letter, or is this the stuff of legend? It doesn't matter, the image still conveys the same urgency. She had made a connection.

34. M. L. Rayne, *What Can a Woman Do?* (Petersburgh, N.Y.: Eagle Publishing Co., 1893; reprint, New York: Arno Press, 1974), p. 408.

Date: Wed, 26 Apr 1995 19:35:46 EDT
To: S.Paige.Baty@williams.edu
From: The Good Man
Subject: Re: NOTEBOOK

Dear Doctor:

At one point you offered to bring your "notebook" to New Orleans, which I assume refers to a small computer thing? Could I take you up on that offer? You told me that yours has a modem and fax built in. You wouldn't happen to know the program/software stuff on there (as you can tell from my vocabulary, I am hopelessly behind the times when it comes to computer things)?

Louisa has a notebook with a built-in modem/fax, and I was hoping we would be able to make yours talk to hers while I'm in NO. The program stuff on hers is COMMWORKS, it has LAPLINK 5 and TS FAX, all on Microsoft Office Programs. Is this what you have on yours? If not, do you know whether or not they could still talk to each other?

See you soon, The Good Man

Love, urgency, and letters form a trinity for those interested in epistles. To write is to feel a need to connect, usually from a distance, with a loved one. If the correspondent is not loved, the letter may serve a separate purpose: reminder of a bill, an invitation to a barbecue, an announcement of a birth. But letters have a history that is linked to love and intimacy. Not all love is romantic. There is a great love between sisters, or sisters and brothers. There is the love between parent and child. There is the love characterized as "Platonic" between two persons of whatever sex. I find the term Platonic odd, as Plato himself is so linked to the sexual—but that is another story, and it's called the *Symposium*. It's really more of a dialogue than a story: kind of like e-mail before computers, when people would have actual conversations in real places. Could Plato's *Republic* have been written in a chat room or on a MUD? We have yet to see; but I merit the guess that the answer is no. Virtual interlocutors just aren't the same. But who knows? Plato could have made the whole thing up anyway. He says himself that he is building a city of words. Why not take him at his word? He made conversation an art. In that famous conversation he made a city called the Republic.

PLATO SAID

"If we watch a city coming into being in words, we may also see its justice and injustice come into being, and when it's finished we should have a better chance of seeing what we're after. Shall we try it that way? Consider this carefully—I think it'll be a lot of work."

"We have," said Adeimantus. "Let's try it."

"Well," I said, "I think a city begins because the individual is not self-sufficient but has many needs. Can you suggest some other origin?"

"No, that's the one."

"So when a number of people have gathered together in one place as common partners and helpers, each inviting others to provide different services (for they have many needs), can we call that settlement a city?"

"Yes," he said. . . .

"Well, then," I said," let's build a city of words from the beginning. It seems it will be created by our needs, of which the most important is providing food for existence and life, next shelter, then clothing, and so on."[35]

How much real communication can take place between a living subject and information disseminated through a computer? Who are the people who write this information, and to whom are they accountable? Is the information superhighway just a bigger version of the Oxford English Dictionary? Can we find knowledge in a piece-meal fashion, or do we need to have a relationship to the source it emanates from? Writing is always about trying to make connections, fixing something in time and place. Information just gives you a fix. The lived art of conversation is dying in much of our world. For awhile I believed it was being reborn in e-mail, or in other places on the Internet. The technology itself has changed the possibilities of connection, but it has also obliterated many of the older ways of communication. I know that it is very different to sit at my small wooden desk and to type this on a powerbook than to write by hand in my journals.

35. Plato, *The Republic*, trans. and ed. Raymond Larson (Arlington Heights, Ill.: AHM Publishing Corp., 1979), p. 41.

The same is true of letters: they obliterate the hand from the correspondence. All the peculiarities of penmanship are gone in this world of virtual letter-writing and information dissemination. In e-mail correspondence what you often get are a bunch of typos and misspelled words, which is I suppose a kind of individual marking, but is not the same thing as a book, or a letter, or a body of works from an author. It is more a random version of someone's *real* self, but it doesn't bear the traces of the writer's hands. It is yet one more morphing of the self brought to you by electronic reproduction. Things like phone calls with terminal screens forcing the speakers to look at each other will change things, too, but not in the way that e-mail has. There are more and more ways to send out words to other people, but these ways do not guarantee any form of connection.

```
Date:    Tue, 25 Apr 1995 19:09:11 CST
To:      s.paige.baty@williams.edu
From:    The Eating Virus
Subject: More Notes About Music and Food

X-Minuet-Version: Minuet1.0_Beta_16
X-Popmail-Charset: English

On Tue, 25 Apr 1995 16:08:36 -0400,
The Good Man wrote:

> Food: Do you really think you're going to get coherent
> information so that you can make some kind of planning
> decision? I didn't think so. The choice is therefore to receive all
> the data (if any comes in) and make an executive decision, and
> therefore have to put up with the whining of the inevitable
> malcontents, or do nothing, and therefore have to put up
> with . . . etc.

Even though it's typical of The Good Man's general view on the
world, my guess is that this instance of pessimism is almost
certainly justified. However, here are two counter-thoughts.
First, Romeo and Juliet have already made their preferences
known in this matter. As will be seen below, there's a fair amount
of congruity between their views. So maybe, just maybe a miracle
will happen and other people will sign on to the same ideas.
Second, anybody who remains silent about these matters will be
considered to have endorsed the decisions of those who speak up.
```

> I'd vote for three nights worth of in-house meals; two relatively
> simple to prepare (soup, sesame noodles) and one night of
> making something fun like pizza.

Sounding a similar note, Juliet said:

> I really like the idea of having some food made to eat at home;
> I particularly like the suggestions of gazpacho and cold sesame
> noodles. Making a big mess in the kitchen is ok too, esp. if that's
> the price for homemade shrimp and crawdad pizza.

So we now have the following food preferences:
    2 votes for a pizza night
    2 votes for cold sesame noodles
    1 vote for gazpacho
    1 vote for some sort of cold soup

Juliet also said:

> Generally I prefer not to spend hours waiting in line for
> restaurants, so I'm voting for eating in or on our feet (at the
> fest) about 3/4 of the time.

That gives us the following on dining locales:
    1 vote for 3 dinners at home and 3 dinners at restaurants
    1 vote for 4-5 dinners at home/fest and 1-2 at restaurants

Juliet also said:

> I also wanted to suggest that we have food on hand for
> breakfast (e.g. bagels, bread, muffins, fruit) because I
> remember that made a big difference in my outlook for the
> day the last time I visited you. I thought maybe we could go
> grocery shopping when we arrive and sort of lay in supplies.

NO, you don't have to vote on this one since it requires no advance
prep on my part. Just an idea for you all to kick around during this
week. As many of you might remember, breakfast is N.O.'s one
major culinary weak point. So I'd say that Juliet's idea makes a
lot of sense to me, especially since the few decent breakfast
places will likely be packed while you're here. It's the price of
coming when there are all these damn tourists in town. Aside to
the Goodman: I know about the guitar thing; I get to it by using
ftp. Aside to Paige: you never told me when you and Leslie are
getting in. How 'bout some flight info? Aside to all: get those
votes in or risk having your lives governed by the decisions of the
Good Man, Juliet and myself. See y'all in a week. Later, Your
friend . . .

WORD SALAD

I confess a predilection for letter-writing as a form of conversation. I like the way it works phenomenologically. I like that it makes a person sit down and write. I don't mean postcards and greeting cards: they are a whole different word game. Anything that comes with a mass-produced message is not a letter: it's a slogan you like and are passing along. Maybe one day we will all simply mail bumper stickers to one another : "I Found It." "Easy Does It." "One Day at a Time." "If you can read this you are too close." Hey, it could work. And think of the extra uses for those stickers: they could be placed on your vehicle, sending letters to everyone on the highway or the freeway or the interstate. You could be a free-floating signifier. "Honk, if you love Jesus."

Geese, not lemmings, flock on the highway. I have gone the way of Mother Goose, as has Technology. For me, it is spirituality and Dr. Seuss. I live in a world of wonder, and dragons, and magic, and princesses, and princes that waken me with a kiss. Then what's amiss, Paige, what's a miss? And still, and still, you must remember this. I am a childless woman who reproduces in other ways. I like to write for fun and play. The magic of my younger days. The city that was San Jose.

stop/hit/nurseryrhyme/key
I am caught up in technology
all my mentors opened doors
left me maps of distant shores
from Poe to Verlaine and Rimbaud
upon a drunken boat I go
Wynken, Blynken, and Nod one night
Went off like three were two
they sailed the seas of sleepless dreams
in a shoehouse built for you
you feasted on those fairy tales
you drank the fairy wine
you woke up dazed, confused, and ill
you longed for the divine

a divine nation we all sought
a union proud and true
three sailors sailed the seas of sky
adrift in a wooden shoe
so I tried to find the prince
and found I'd kissed the toad
silly rhymes and pies that mince
simple timing with the code

Here is the code. It is a postal code. Stamp your feet. It is icy on the steps. Nothing can stop the U.S. male. He will persist and persist until you have lost yourself to him, forgotten who you were before he woke you up with a letter or a seal or a kiss and saved your life. These are the dreams you were taught to dream as a child:

Sleeping Beauty
Cinderella
Snow White
Rapunzel
East of the Sun, West of the Moon
Rumpelstiltskin
Thumbelina

I too once dreamt these dreams, although I read other books. Once, when I asked my mother for a fairy tale, she gave me Kafka's *The Castle*. I was eleven years old. She was getting divorced from my father. I loved that fairy tale, and wanted to read more of the same. My tastes turned to Tolstoy, Camus, Steinbeck, Hemingway, Fitzgerald, Saint-Exupéry, and Flaubert. I was a wreck, but I loved it. Still, now I ask, where were the women? Sure I read *Gone with the Wind* and *Little Women* and books by E. Nesbit, but in my youth I never met Gertrude Stein, Joan Didion, Virginia Woolf, Margaret Fuller, Kate Chopin, Willa Cather, Flannery O'Connor, or anyone else. I met them at Smith College, a college for women, and still there we met only on occasion.

Usually I was reading the entire works of Plato, Nietzsche, D. H. Lawrence, Aristotle, Mill, Hobbes, Locke, and Paine. But sometimes there were women. I tried to find out about the relationship between wisdom and love in these texts, but mostly I was just perplexed. I wanted to make a connection. I wanted to get a fix on things. I made up lists to figure it all out, but always ended up where I began in the first place: with a list of people I couldn't fix at all. Nothing had one meaning for me. I wanted to know what love meant, and how it related to writing.

What kinds of love can be found in writing, letters, and conversation? The love between a student and a teacher. The love between Plato and Socrates. The love between Romeo and Juliet. The love between Karl Jaspers and Hannah Arendt. The love between Susan B. Anthony and Elizabeth Cady Stanton. The love between Griffin and Sabine. The love between Usbek and himself. The love between Harriet Taylor and John Stuart Mill. The love between Napoleon and Josephine. The love between Nathaniel Hawthorne and Sophia Peabody. The love between Mary and Jesus. The love between Jesus and Mary Magdalene. The love between Maggie and Hopey. The love between me and my mother. The love between me and my friends. The love between Goethe and Bettina. The love between Louisa May Alcott and Ralph Waldo Emerson, which was based upon Louisa's early reading of Bettina and Goethe's relationship. The love between me and Speedy. The love I feel for Jack. The love I feel for Orestes. The love for my sisters, and my brother. My love for Dr. Jung. There are many ways of loving, and they do not all involve king/queen pairings. Beware of love that leads to false forms of connection and domination. Real love and correspondence is about reciprocity, community, understanding, and forgiveness. It has in itself a history. History does not mean that the story is over: it means that the story is rooted in real experience, and that it has the possibility to change and grow. Here is a story about love and community.

THE MAIL BOX: A STORY ABOUT
LOUISA MAY ALCOTT

Gloria T. Delamar, author of *Louisa May Alcott and "Little Women,"*
tells it this way about Louisa May:

*She was inspired, too, by her adoration of Ellen's father, the kind,
illustrious Emerson. To this friend she was deeply attached.
Inspired by the romantic books of Goethe, she wrote secret love
letters to Emerson which she never mailed, and left wildflowers
on his doorstep. She sat in a tall cherry tree at midnight to
serenade him with German love songs, sung so softly he never
knew she was under his window. "He is my idol," she sighed.
Beside his kindnesses to her, she knew that it was he who so
frequently left discreet gifts of money on their mantle under a
candlestick or tucked into a book.*[36]

In real life, which is a hard term to use at any time and particularly in relationship to Louisa May Alcott, who made of her life a
glorious fiction, letters were sent in love and confidence, or remained
unsent, as in the relationship between the older Emerson and the
girl Louisa. In her day-to-day life Miss Alcott corresponded with hosts
of friends, ranging from Lydia Maria Child to Ellen Emerson to her
sisters to her publishers, and the list goes on. Abba May Alcott,
Louisa's mother, had created a post office box for the girls to post
letters to one another and their neighbors, the Emersons. Here is an
account of a similar letterbox from Alcott's novel *Little Women*:

*I merely wish to say, that as a slight token of my gratitude for the
honor done me, and as a means of promoting friendly relations
between adjoining nations, I have set up a post-office in the
hedge in the lower corner of the garden; a fine, spacious building,
with padlocks on the doors, and every convenience for the
mails—also the females, if I may be allowed the expression. It's
the old martin-house; but I've stopped up the door, and made the
roof open, so it will hold all sorts of things, and save our valuable*

36. Gloria T. Delamar,
*Louisa May Alcott
and "Little Women"*
(Jefferson, N.C.:
McFarland and Co.,
1990), p. 32.

*time. Letters, manuscripts, books, and bundles can be passed in
there; and, as each nation has a key, it will be uncommonly nice,
I fancy.*[37]

Correspondence with every convenience for the mails, and also
for the females: an early version of e-mail trouble. Mail is gendered
both ways at once in this gentler passage, but as the March girls
troop into young womanhood the box will transform. While it all
begins innocently, the box will later become the receptacle of love
letters between "Meg" and "John." What is it about the mail that
lends itself to a lover's discourse? What is it that takes us from sending "manuscripts, books, and bundles" to emotional baggage
through the mail? And what other things do we send? Illicit sub-
stances, bombs, hate-mail, angry protests to the editor? Is correspondence about honesty or lies? Is correspondence about love or
hate or need or quiet desperation? What have you posted lately?
Why do you send letters? Do you have a box of letters from loves
lost, or keepsakes from loves present? What do you treasure in these
letters? Are they the same as e-mail messages you've saved on your
prosthetic memory? Shakespeare knew about letters and love and
how they figured in plots. If only the messenger had arrived earlier,
Romeo and Juliet would not have had to die. Kill the messenger. Kill
the sender. Return to sender. Melville knew about dead letters and
what they signify in our culture: messages of life, speeding on errands of death; and we, Bartlebys all, hoping to receive the right
message. Dearest, I await thee. I have come for thee. You know not
the hour of my coming, but I send you a letter as a promise, as a
bridge. Dearest, I adore thee: dearest I implore thee. Could you be
my one this time? Will you be my valentine?

Maybe Valentine's Day should be abolished. Maybe we should
make every day Valentine's Day. Maybe we should stop dreaming
up fairy-tale romances and start at the beginning in the garden. In
the garden, where everything was beautiful and perfect and had a
place and order and name. Maybe we should destroy all mail-order
catalogues. Maybe we should pass a law that all letters must be
immediately burnt upon their writing or after reception. Maybe we

37. Louisa May
Alcott, *Little Women*,
Ch. 10 (New York:
A. L. Burt and Co.,
1910, published by
arrangement with
Little, Brown, and
Co., from 1868 ed.),
p. 91.

should save all correspondence. Maybe we can make a happily-ever-after ending. But are endings ever happy? Or is it just the beginnings that we crave, from the cradle to the grave? Beginnings can seem easy because they momentarily allow us to forget our history. But our history follows us wherever we go, and in every new beginning there will be contained the shapes and textures of the history that made this beginning happen. Some beginnings are a good thing, but others are based on bad faith. Any beginning that has not fully reckoned with history is doomed to failure. There can be no true correspondence: people, including you, will be hurt or lost in the process of forgetting yourself and the people that have made you who you are. When you are confused you look for beginnings that allow you to escape your past, but there is no escaping the world you made for yourself with other people. Wherever you go, there you are. And where you are, these people will be with you. E-mail trouble happened because I was confused, searching for a beginning I didn't really want as I was desperately trying to escape myself and my history. I thought that I could make a temporary connection with virtual strangers, but this didn't work. I was not fully reckoning with my history.

Where was I? Oh yes, on my way to the city of the crescent moon, New Orleans. At the last minute I was able to persuade my sister Leslie to accompany me on my journey to meet the Good Man and his virtual friends. Her presence was the saving grace of my short-lived season in e-mail. We were excited about the trip. We had on our nice clothes. The woman on the plane thought we were in a band, and so we said that we were. "What are you called?" she asked. "Bad Hair Day," I replied. She smiled and said that she had heard of us. After this we drank some Finlandia vodka and got more and more excited about the trip. We were going to somebody else's "Big Chill," and we didn't know what it would be like. If worse came to worse, we reasoned, we could go somewhere else. We didn't count on all the hotels being full. We didn't count on a lot of things, because even after our thirty-something odd years of life we thought that most people were nice. Besides, I had this "relationship" with the Goodman. He was kind, and we spoke often. I had confessed to him that I was very nervous about meeting him in the flesh. "Don't worry," he said, "I'm a nice guy." He seemed like one on the terminal, then eventually on the phone: he had a nice phone voice. (Things progressed from one form of virtual connection to another.) How bad could it be?

Pretty bad. We arrived at the airport and called their home to find an answering machine message advising us to take a cab to an obscure sandwich shop. And so we did, only when we got there we didn't know who to look for. We sat, confounded, in the cab. A man walked up to my door. "You must be Paige," he said. "I am the good man." I shook his hand. I was a bit the worse for it after the vodka on the plane, but I was still clear-headed. Nonetheless, after the Good Man sat down with his friends, these people put me off. We sat down and they ignored us. They ate their food and spoke among themselves. Not once did the good man make eye contact with me. When I tried to speak to him, he would politely turn away. I was growing more and more confused. We left in a minivan to our host's apartment. Things went from awkward to worse. They were drinking lots of pricey whiskey and acting like we were not there. They showed us to our room. "What's up with these guys?" Leslie wondered. She already wanted out. We thought it might improve when we all went out to hear some music, but there we did not trip the light fantastic. We all just sort of sat separately and drank in silence. Leslie tried to buy our host a drink. "I'll get it myself," he told her. (We later learned that he was not the host, but the host's brother. For the first two days they lied about who was who and switched names on us. It was like a role-playing game without any of the fun. Or if there was fun it was at our expense.)

Hi all. Before getting to the question of food and crankiness
One of our friends wrote:

> 1) New Orleans features some of the finest dining
> establishments in the nation, and the regional cuisine is world
> renowned.

Did anybody disagree with this? I don't think so. My questions
continue to be:

1) Do you all want to eat out every night, or would you prefer
to eat in some nights.

If the latter, I add the following question:

a) Would you all like me to pre-prepare some foods prior to
your arrival?

If the answer to that is yes, I add the following questions:

i) Roughly how many nights would you like me to
prepare foods for? and

ii) What foods would you like me to prepare? Remember,
the idea is to make things ahead of time that will keep
ready to eat in the fridge. So far beet soup, gazpacho
and sesame noodles have received votes. If people want
Gumbo it can be bought at the fairgrounds, at Brennans,
at Franky and Johnny's, at Jaeger's, at The Gumbo Shop,
at The Praline Connection, at Madigan's and so on,
although not at Ghenghis Khan's. If people want, we
could spend several hours making gumbo. However, the
fact is, I'm not offering to cook that ahead of time. It's
too much work, and there are too many places around
here that do it at least as well as I would, especially
since it'd be chilled and reheated prior to eating. So that
puts us back at the question of whether you all would
like me to prepare some things that are good straight
out of the fridge. Got it?

> 2) Fuck this group ethic and go solo.

A fine idea. I'd add that we could also all go to the same
restaurants, but split up into smaller groups thereby enabling us
to be more quickly seated. My questions raised above still stand.

> It may just turn out that one week of close quarters and strong
> personalities will create enough friction within our group of
> 10-12 to ignite Lake Pontchartrain.

Huh? Strong personalities? Friction? In our group? When? Where?
You must have us confused with some other group.

> Question: Does raw oysters and beer at Ajax constitute a meal,
> a snack, or simply a way to kill time?
> 3) "Breakfast at Brennan's" was the whole reason Andrew
> Jackson made the Louisiana Purchase.

Setting aside the already-corrected historical inaccuracy in
the above statement, I only add the following: if you (or anybody
else for that matter) are willing to pick up the tab, I'll gladly
breakfast at Brennan's every morning while you're here;
otherwise, not.

> Cafe Du Monde? Coffee, donuts, and entertainment, 24 hours a
> day.

True, but no biscuits, no grits, no eggs, no waffles, no english
muffins, no pancakes, no pecan pie, not even bagels are available
there. CDM is a fine place to go for a break in between the daquiri
shop and the Acme, but it's not a great breakfast spot.
86: Mother's, 401 Poydras Street. Grits and andouille sausage.
Popular and populist.
This is a very special place. It's down in the CBD. Last time I was
there I had a calamari po' boy; something I've seen on no other
menu in town. I'll look into their hours. If we get there early
enough to beat the crowd of lunch-seeking office workers, we
should do okay in terms of waiting (unless, of course, the tourists
have also found out about it (which they might have given its
publicity in Travel & Leisure)). BTW this place doesn't do tables: it's
cafeteria style, and when you've got your food, you find a place
to eat it.

> Bagels? What, are you from New York? Can you say biscuits and
> grits? I can, and I'm there.

Crazy idea, I know, but as Jimmy so wisely said, "Fuck this group
ethic."

We returned to the crowded apartment, and my sister and I shared
a bed. (Out of fairness I should say that our host gave up his own
bed and slept on the floor for the duration of our stay, and that was
an act of generosity. He was, on the whole, a generous person.)

Date: Thu, 27 Apr 1995 10:00:05 EDT
To: pbaty@williams.edu and the e-mail virtual circle
cc: Whining Po' Boy Grad Student
          Supreme Exhaulted Leader
          Should be defending O.J.
          Potential Babe Action <s.paige.baty@williams.edu>,
          Personal Sex Slave @juliet.
From: Mr. Right
Subject: Make me a pallet on you floor

Is it suggested that we bring some sort of bed roll, sleeping bag,
or hammock of our own?
Crankpot

Conversation was forced. The group of men—who numbered
four—had all been friends in college. They reverted to their old ways
of being; basically telling a lot of sex jokes or using bathroom humor.

I didn't care, but I felt weird because our e-mail exchanges had
been so different. On the terminal and on the phone, we talked
about life and death and books and love and our feelings and our
days and what we had made for dinner. In person, we did not talk.
They spoke, and the women were virtually silent: we didn't even
talk of Michelangelo. We just came and went.

Date: Thu, 27 Apr 1995 09:55:57 CST
To: s.paige.baty@williams.edu and the virtual circle
From: @mailhost
Subject: Re: Make me a pallet on you floor

On Thu, 27 Apr 1995 10:00:05 -0400,
Mr. Write wrote:

> Is it suggested that we bring some sort of bed roll, sleeping bag,
> or hammock of our own?

I am hurt. Nay, insulted. You, Mr. Write, who have not only seen
the spacious accommodations of _La_Villa_-- _, but who have
also known my generous ways as a host for many a year, you ask
such a question as this? Do you think I would deny you any of the
vast comforts of my home? Of course I wouldn't. You are welcome
to any space on the living or dining room floor that you would like
(unless, of course, somebody else stakes it out before you do).
There is also the couch. Perhaps you will be the first to lay a claim
to that. Perhaps not. Um, so, in a word, the answer to your
questions is, yes. In the next couple of days I'll send around a
fuller list of suggested items to bring.
Any other questions?

The thing is, in a certain way, we really liked those guys. One of them had a deadpan sense of life and humor that left me laughing out of my gut in a way that I had not done in a long time. And another one was just plain nice to me and my sister the whole time— bought us dinner, talked to us, was full of daily kindnesses. I don't quite know why the whole operation got botched. If I place the blame anywhere, it is with myself and e-mail trouble. Maybe I just went in with the wrong set of expectations, and these made me overlook all of the good that was there. Looking backward, I see the good. I see that it was probably really weird for them too. I was not exactly the easiest person in the world for those few daze, because of where I'd come from and where I hadn't been. This city signified too heavily for me. My father had died there only six months before, and we had to go through his things and decide what to keep and to throw away and if he should be buried or cremated, and in the end he was burnt and put into a very beautiful military grave at Arlington because he fought in the Navy.

There were too many ghosts for me in New Orleans, and maybe this is why one of the men called me "an energy vampire." I don't think he meant it in a bad way, but it hit hard. I was trying to tell the story of getting a cab ride in the blinding rain—which I learned was not a metaphor, but a statement of truth about rain under some circumstances—and what the cabdriver told me. I was excited, and I talked and talked and they stared at me as if I were a stranger. I *was* the stranger. I was talking about how the man who drove the cab wanted to be a lawyer, but in those times in the south for black folk there was no money for him so he told me the Mississippi River became his mother and father and he was a longshoreman and he wanted to go to college but the river couldn't send him there. He kept on moving, anyway. Now he was a cabdriver, who knew a Southerner when he saw one. He told me the whole story of his life, and he gave me his card. He had bought a bar, and his partner was named "Lawyer." He told me he figured it for the next best thing. He had five kids and almost all of them went to college and now two were teachers and at his bar there was red beans and rice on Wednesdays, and blues on Thursdays, and crawfish on Fridays, and disco for the young folks on Saturdays. He wanted me to go to the bar with him that night; said he'd come back for me, and I wanted to go. But I had previous engagements, so I never saw him again. He was one of the best connections I made during that trip. I told him how I had come to be there, and he took it all in through a long Southern pause and said to my sister, "Sounds like there is a love problem she is leaving out of this story." He was right, as most Southerners tend to be on such things. They are good storytellers, and even better listeners, even if they do interrupt constantly. If you grow up Southern, you learn to talk on top of everyone else at the same time. This is how it is for me with my family, who are Southern. I am surrounded by Southerners who miss home; but that time down South I did not feel at home; I felt like a nervous stranger, except when I would walk in the night with my sister alone and show her the mysteries of the city and it was good and we were good and the town was our mother and father.

CUT/PASTE/LOVE'S BODY IN NEW ORLEANS

The cave of dreams and the cave of the dead are the same cave. Ghosts are dreams, and dreams are ghosts: shades, umbrae. *Sleep is regressive; in dreaming we return to dream time—the age of heroes and ancestors; Roheim's* Eternal Ones of the Dream; *or the primal parents. In the idea of reincarnation, the father finds his child in a dream: i.e., finds the child pre-existent, in spirit or ancestral form; in some cave or water hole.*[38]

Remember, I was at that time stuck in the matrix, the cave. I was searching for my dead father, and trying not to bleed. I was looking for God. I was looking for a good man. I couldn't find any of that trinity, I just saw signs of lost infinity. The city was bleeding into nothingness for me, just like everything else. But at the end of the dream I confronted the real, abruptly. I found my father and the son and myself. I was still a lonesome traveler, but somehow it didn't

38. Brown, *Love's Body,* p. 46.

matter in the same way anymore. There were some good dreams in that city, before I woke up. In one of those dreams I went to Lafitte's Pirate Bar and sang with the eighty-year-old guy who's been playing for years and Leslie had on her Nana Jane's outfit and a Frenchman said to her that Nana Jane was very happy that night and we stayed out late and we knew some joy and we knew some music and we got lost in that moment.

After four days we thought we had to get out of that house, because a lot of things had happened and we didn't feel we should be there and my sister could not sleep, and this girl I used to know said why didn't we stay with some of her friends who lived in the city. We left during the day when the virtual circle was out hearing music. I left each one of them a yellow Post-it Note on their luggage, and in the case of the host, on the refrigerator. I said, "Thank you." I said, "I'm sorry." I said, "It did not work out." We felt like Thelma and Louise, fleeing some unknown force, and it wasn't even them, but we had to get out. I left the good man a Post-it Note telling him that I hated abrupt endings. I wondered if he could tell me why things went the way they did. I told him that my father had died without so much as a fare you well, and that I was living it again. I asked if he could e-mail or phone or write and explain why he had systematically erased me. He never answered the Post-it Note, and I do not now expect an answer. I do not believe he had an answer. He had told me I was fighting my own demons, and he was right. He was not the demon I had to fight. He knew about battle cries: Ya Ya Henna! He was just tired and didn't want to do battle with me. In the long run I can't say that I blame him at all. I am simply grateful for the brief period when we appeared to correspond. I am writing you: Good-bye. Fight your demons with courage and honor. Sorry that you got caught in my Tennessee Williams script of a life. And thanks for the education. As you said, it was something I knew anyway, only I was in denial.

Why do women apologize at the end? I don't know, but today it feels good to do it. This is an apologia. Go look it up in the OED. Or maybe you should just read some of the personals ads that you can find in any city around this country and you'll get an idea of what

I'm getting at. It was a hoooooop dance. I was the white? girl dancing. I had no idea where I was heading when I left that house but believeyoume it was not a peaceful place. It was to the home of these two characters who had a pretty scary relationship to reality. They were kind of sort of psychotic brilliant wired angry drunken people bent on self-destruction. The first night at their house, which was a beautiful old New Orleans of a place, we ate crawfish on the porch with our new host's mother and she talked on and on into the night as Southern women are wont to do. She was a kind and good woman. There was a lot of unspoken and spoken tension there. At my new place of residence it was not about being erased, it was about racing.

I had landed my sister in a house of a woman and a man who had crashed hard in life and made a habit out of new and better ways of crashing. It was a house with a lot of arguments and broken windows and threats and love and demons that were not at all hidden. These people led lives of very noisy desperation. After about four hours there it was clear to me that we were in a bad way. I began to plot ways out, but all the hotels were still full and we didn't know how to leave without making things worse. We watched them fight and we watched them curse. We took a break and went the next day down to the river: it was my mother and father that day, too. I thought about the cabdriver and my father and sang with my sister a bunch of Dylan tunes plus Southern stuff like "What a Friend We Have in Jesus." The girl we were staying with told me I had a Jesus complex. After two days there I told her that if I ever wished I were Jesus, it was right then because I wanted to lay my hands on her and heal her. I was not Jesus, so I just couldn't do it. Instead, I gave her one of my shirts that she liked. I hope it gives her some kind of cover or shelter or something good. It was a gift given freely, and I genuinely liked that girl. It was just that she was so sad and broken and angry and I did not know what else I could do.

My sister and I decided to take the two of them out to dinner at my favorite New Orleans restaurant, the "Praline Connection." Maybe the food and conversation would save us. We all trooped down there; or rather, they met us at a bar because we were playing pool with some really nice kids who had come from military families in D.C. and recently moved to New Orleans. They were good pool players, and young, and we played with them for about four hours while we waited for our new hosts to show up for dinner, and they finally did but they were already acting weird, and so we left our names on the list and had a drink at the bar across the street that felt and looked as if somebody had just come in and cleared everything out of a gigantic Laundromat and put a little bar in the corner, and it was like a lemonade stand made by children but it was pricey, and outside it started raining hard. My sister was freezing, because she was wet and cold, and so the guy we were staying with let her wear his jacket. In a while we got our table.

About halfway through the dinner the storm was so bad that all the lights went out and they came and lit candles and people tried to get cabs but it turned out to be impossible because something like eighteen inches of water fell in three hours and big sections of the city were several feet underwater. We were stuck in the French Quarter and it was the witching hour and so we did the only thing we could do, which was go to a bar to get out of the blinding rain and wait till it might be possible to get home. The same kids were still there, playing pool. At this point the guy we were staying with had had so many double Jim Beams that he just passed out on a table and we left him there for a good few hours and his girlfriend started freaking out at my sister for wearing his coat. She had this whole thing going on in her head that my sister was trying to get her boyfriend, which was crazy, and so she started threatening to kick Leslie's ass and Leslie just starting weeping and the poor military kids who liked us didn't know what to do, but I told them to keep out of it because this woman was pretty dangerous when she was off on a trip and I tried to talk her into leaving with me and just let Leslie stay and play pool and I'd buy her a drink somewhere else.

I eventually did this, and we end up in some weird bar where there is still no electricity like everywhere else in the city that night and these guys are playing harp and hollow body guitar blues and I'm worrying about Leslie and thinking about my brother and then the girl insists that we have to go back and get her passed-out boyfriend and Leslie and try to get home or to make them hear these blues, which were no good to be blunt about it. After what was almost a physical argument we did go get them and take them to the bar.

After two more hours or so I had to leave no matter what, and was not leaving my sister at this point, so we went outside, where the bartender said we were taking our lives in our hands because there was a lot of looting and the city had gone crazy. Sure enough, the first thing we see is this group of kids in like rayon silver post-eighties mock-seventies clothes shooting guns out in the street and laughing, and they come up to us, so I drag the passed-out guy back in the first bar, where the same nice kids are playing pool, and it's now like four in the morning and we all just sit down to wait it out. A guy with a hook for an arm comes in off the street and accuses me of stealing his small, black film case which has his stash of crack. No, I have never seen this guy, but he is crazy and his hook is sharp-looking and there is no talking normal to him and the girl starts screaming at him and it gets physical and I decide I am getting the hell out of there, with Leslie, who is now drunk, no matter what it takes me, so I tell them they can follow or not but we are walking. We walk fast in the pouring rain and there is wreckage everywhere and it floats by us the further we get in the flood and somehow the two of them are keeping up like a block behind and we walk for about half an hour and make it to Canal Street which is several feet underwater, but we are alive and everyone is kind of crazy and happy by now because it is the apocalypse.

Canal Street is awash in cars, with drivers sitting on the tops because their engines have flooded, literally. Everyone is drunk and still drinking because all the bars and liquor stores are open and there is nothing else to do and no one can get home and they have all given up on it. We walk down the street in about two or three feet of water and we are laughing and fish are going by our legs and we are soaking wet and then this weird thing happens where one solemn boat of a car comes driving by and for some reason this car can make it through the flood and the guy offers us a ride and I say, "no way," but the other three pile in and being the loyal sort who cannot abandon my sister to death I reluctantly get in, insisting on a seat by the door in the back. After about a minute it is clear to me the guy is 100 percent crazy because he claims he was a cop and now works for some secret military service and he has locked all the doors and windows with this electric device in the front and he just gets in this weird rap and offers us all beers, which I don't take because I figure they are drugged. I'm looking for some way out, and it's still like forty blocks home but when we get to a street about twenty blocks away the guy says, "no, not here," and won't stop and puts on *Peter Frampton Comes Alive* and I figure we are in for it now as two of us are passed out and the third is crazy so it is me versus the driver, and I start thinking about possible weapons.

Suddenly, we are saved by the flood because a huge wave of water comes up Canal and even this über-car can't make it anymore and I say "Unlock the door" and he says, "No," so I smash my hand through the window and open it from outside and he is swearing at me and calling me crazy and I am dragging my sister into the dark flood and somehow the other two get out 'cause the driver is pissed and maybe doesn't want to bother anymore or figures he has run into a group as crazy as the cluster of personalities that make up himself. I ask them where the house is and they are laughing and drunk and marveling at the water and Leslie is coming around and we start walk-swimming through these streets just laughing and shouting and people all on their porches surveying the wreckage of their cars and gardens and lives and there are so many live things from the river and we just keep going further and people wave to us and it's a crazy dream and we finally get to the house which is flooded up to the porch and two people have left their cars on the lawn and they are covered in water. We get inside after rescuing the cat who is trapped under the house on a beam. Part of the roof over our bed has come down and everything inside is wet and I say we will sleep on the wooden floor at this point because there are no blankets, sheets, nothing dry, not even a towel; but they are all of a sudden kind and insist on our splitting their bed in half and us sleeping on the box springs in the one dry room which is the front one that a guy tried breaking into the night before. It is too much work to argue so

I say okay and it's another half hour before the bed is remade and Leslie falls asleep and I am up and trying to figure how to get out for good. The street is impassable, so I figure we will just leave all of our stuff. I don't care anymore, except about this one coat that I plan to take. I know a bad situation when I am in it. I decide to wait till it's eight or nine A.M., and let myself sleep for an hour and a half.

When I wake up the phone is ringing and it is our host's Southern mother and she says that she will find a way to get us and take us to the airport and that if she had anything to do with it we never would have been there and she tells me this is the worst flood in five hundred years and that there are billions of dollars in damage, and a lot of that is in all the wrecked cars. They are trying to pump out the street and she ends up showing up in a car and we somehow make it to the airport, even though all over the place the only things we see are people on cars, and flooded-out sections of the highway, and whole neighborhoods underwater if you look down from the freeway. She drops us at the airport and we are so relieved because all we plan on doing is leaving in one hour and the man at the desk says no planes out that day and maybe not for a few more because the runway is several feet underwater and the airline won't pay for the hotel because over ten thousand people are stuck there and I get mad, and then try acting nice when I remember maybe he has lost his house or something. He then gives us a discount pass to a cheap hotel by the airport, where we finally arrive and wait out the rest of the storm. The staff there is overworked because no one can get in or out so some of them have been working now for maybe three days and we get a second-floor room because a lot of the first floor is underwater and we sit and we watch a television and it is the first time I like TV after so many months because it means there is electricity and also a world out there. I want to go back home. I use the phone to try and make a connection, but phones cannot save you from the apocalypse. By this time I just want out of the deluge. I want to live in a world which is not about fantasy, crashing, and floods. I want to be in a clean, well-lighted place. That place is with someone who knows me and knows my history. That place is not this place: a world of disconnection and insanity.

I switch to CNN and there is no coverage of the flood. The only place we can find news about it is the one local channel, but they mostly run a lot of M*A*S*H, with occasional updates on flooding, and pictures of whole towns like Slidell under water. We can finally use a phone so I call to say that I am stuck in this terrible flood and can't get back to teach and that sort of thing, and then we get some food and watch TV and don't talk, but are just relieved, and want home. In two more days we get home and we have no ride because it was unclear when we would get in and we have this taxi driver who starts explaining all the local flora and fauna to us, and tells us about her girlfriend, who is a pop singer and also from Cuba. We like her because she lets us smoke in the cab. It is a $100 cab ride home. I pay her off, and we stumble into our place, and I realize that I have to teach the next day, and I am so exhausted and suddenly in a reality where no-one-else-at-all just lived through the apocalypse but Leslie, who will respond by not getting out of bed for a number of days. The whole story seems too crazy to repeat so I just wake up the next morning and I teach Pynchon's *The Crying of Lot 49* and it is the last day of classes @ williams.edu.

The students are annoyed that I appear to have skipped out on class two days ago, but what kind of an explanation could I give them? I was stuck in the apocalypse, but it never made the news, so I say I was out of town and that has to do for an explanation.

Date: Thu, 04 May 1995 13:01:00 EDT
To: S.Paige.Baty@williams.edu
From: ATP last WEEKEND!!! <@williams.edu>
Subject: many things

paige,
      i'm sorry that i have missed class again today. i generally don't feel comfortable giving excuses, but i have been under a tremendous amount of stress lately, and have been pulling near-all-nighters at least every other day for the past week or so. i hope you understand. i am still trying to keep up with the reading, and i will not miss any more classes.

as of yet, i still have not handed in my first & second paper. i wish to combine the two. my project, a comic strip, has been inches from completion for at least 2 or so weeks. the way i have handled this situation is near ridiculous. i have been wanting to meet personally with you for the longest time, but scheduling due to my class schedule as well as the (very successful!) asian-american theatre production, jurasian park, and various asian-american heritage month activities (i have helped organize many events, mcc lunch forums, as well as activism towards the few asian-american hunger strikes across the nation) have delayed our meeting. looking clearly at why i wanted to speak with you, i realize that perhaps the best way is over e-mail.

previously, i had also wanted to discuss with you whether my thinking and views towards the authors we have studied were correct and interpretable through the comic media. i wish i could have actively worked with you in this area, but again, scheduling conflicts.
i hope to hear from you soon. i apologize that i have made this process of handing in this one paper so long and drawn out. it's just that i wanted this paper to be done so well, but was ineffective in doing so.

i would also like to thank you for letting me into this course at the beginning of the semester. i was a drop/add student. i'd like to think that i would be the same person that i am now without this course, but i doubt it. courses like this are very important, especially to those students like myself who are considering majoring in the sciences as well as being pre-med. with that curriculum in mind, it is very easy to overlook things such as political and social theory in light of one's ultimate goals and careers. i am glad that i have taken this course; i feel that i have developed much more personally and intellectually from the readings and your lectures. thank you.

apologizing for the length,
a student of politics

So it is the last day of class and I decide to focus on Inamorati Anonymous, because it most resonates with the virtual reality I've been living for the past few days and months and years, really. Here is the story of Inamorati Anonymous, by Thomas Pynchon, who is another dead author who has made a science out of being the invisible man, or the indivisible man, or what have you. He even had someone else sit for his Cornell yearbook photo. I didn't need to do that because I change the way I look so often half of the time my own family does not recognize me. On the other hand, now I have a couple of distinguishing marks that will be more difficult to conceal should I wish to make myself invisible to those around me. I will worry about that later. (Not all the Southern scripts are gone.)

INAMORATI ANONYMOUS: A STORY BY
A DEAD AUTHOR

On her crazy journey in San Francisco Ms. Oedipa Maas ends up at a bar called The Greek Way, wearing an I.D. that names her as "Arnold Snarb." She espies a man wearing a muted post horn on his lapel, the sign of Trystero, or whatever it is, that she has been seeking. She approaches him for answers. After a bit of debate the conversation goes like this:

"And," scratching the stubble on his head, "you have nobody else to tell this to. Only somebody in a bar whose name you don't know?"

She wouldn't look at him. "I guess not."

"No husband, no shrink?"

"Both," Oedipa said, "but they don't know."

"You can't tell them?"

She met his eyes' void for a second after all, and shrugged.

"I'll tell you what I know, then," he decided. "The pin I'm wearing means I'm a member of the IA. That's Inamorati Anonymous. An inamorato is somebody in love. That's the worst addiction of all."[39]

That's what it all comes down to, at a certain point in the evening. A woman ends up in a bar called The Greek Way, and is searching for answers. She meets a man who tells her that "love is the worst addiction of all." She is open to correspondence. She has been tracking W.A.S.T.E., the alternative mail route, via which a number of other Americans appear to correspond with one another. The correspondence is all about disconnection, or missed connections. W.A.S.T.E. is the system of entropy, or the mechanism of alternative connection. Love and mail are about these forms of connection and disconnection, as is the Greek way. Oedipa, being a lonesome traveler, wants to know more from the man whose name she doesn't know, and so he tells her all he has to say on this subject:

Inamorati Anonymous is a system of disconnection set up by a failed suicide, or fallen upon by a failed suicide, depending on how

39. Thomas Pynchon, *The Crying of Lot 49* (New York: Bantam Books, 1967), pp. 82–83.

you look upon it. They do not hold meetings: theirs is an organization based upon being invisible to other members. As the man says, "We're isolates, Arnold. Meetings would destroy the whole point of it." A society of isolates, who get somebody dispatched to them through an answering service that makes sure no two people meet more than twice, for fear that some form of feeling might develop between them. The society has a secret history, and here is how it goes:

In the early 1960's a Yoyodyne executive living near L.A. is fired, or replaced, because his job can be done by a computer. As he is unused to making any decisions without the help of a committee, he places an ad in the personals of the L.A. *Times*, "asking whether anyone who'd been in the same fix ever found any good reasons for not committing suicide." He assumes that he will receive no replies, as the suicides will all be dead, and he'd only receive thereby an affirmation through absence. He is wrong. After waiting a few days, a man appears at his door with a bag of letters. They are all from failed suicides; but the thing is, none of them can come up with any good reasons for still living. He decides to kill himself, and so stuffs his pockets with these letters and gets ready to torch himself like the Buddhist Monk he reads about in the newspaper who set himself on fire to protest the war. Just as he is about to set himself aflame, he is startled by voices. His wife and the efficiency expert who had him fired are about to have sex in his living room, on the carpet. They come upon him.

"I was about to do the Buddhist Monk thing," explained the executive. "Nearly three weeks it takes him," marvelled the efficiency expert, "to decide. You know how long it would've taken the IBM 7094? Twelve microseconds. No wonder you were replaced."[40]

The executive begins to laugh, and cannot stop laughing. He has met Buddha on the road, and he decides not to kill himself. He takes it as a sign, after he sees the muted post horn on the back of the stamps of the letters from the other failed suicides. He decides to

40. Pynchon, *The Crying of Lot 49*, p. 85.

swear off all love of other humans, animals, cars, and everything else. He declares himself the founder of a society of isolates. Oedipa wants to hear more, and is told by the stranger to write the founder through W.A.S.T.E.

"Think of it," he went on, also drunk, "A whole underworld of suicides who failed. All keeping in touch through that secret delivery system. What do they tell each other?"[41]

We are in the classroom analyzing this exchange of meaning. What does it mean, or should we bother asking? Are we asking the right questions? I will warn you right now that this is not about final solutions, just puzzling things over. Oedipa's journey does not end there; this is just the story of one of her encounters on the journey. She is trying to make connections, and gets a history that is founded upon disconnection and death and failure. To be a failed suicide is perhaps the best and worst thing to be. What would it mean to be a successful suicide? Well, the answer should be sort of obvious, but maybe not, depending on how you read the book and what you mean by suicide. To be a failed suicide would be an all-too-human condition, it appears. The failed suicides swear off the world, but they still connect through the system of disconnection that is W.A.S.T.E. It was too much connection that made them want to die in the first place. Now they are living out lives that are virtual suicides.

E-mail is kin to I.A.; only people get to make a lot of connections with the same person again and again if they so choose. These connections require absence. These connections are about not being there. These connections are about love, or longing, or a kind of love that both demands to be heard and requires a space for pouring itself out, like so much gasoline, on the screen of the recipient. This is not real love. This is projection. This is about the foreign territory of the id. This is about a society of isolates who all communicate with one another from terminal sites. This is about being disembodied, distanced, distinct, and that sort of boundary-thing. It is not about being present. It is not about being there. It is not about a

41. Ibid.

shared history, or a shared meal, or a shared story, or any kind of mutuality. It is about contact between virtual strangers. There is no exchange of bodily fluids on the Internet. It is the kind of connection that occurs when you have become entirely without ground, when you have no husband, no shrink, no buffers to keep you safe in the world. It happens when you feel that you are so alone that you need anybody to talk to—anybody at all—because you believe that your connections have failed you. This kind of connection leaves you cold and dead inside, because it lacks history and a language of belonging.

Date: Mon., 27 Feb. 1995 16:17:07 EST
To: S.Paige.Baty@williams.edu
From: the death of speedy
Subject: sorry

i'm beginning to worry that some of my stuff overlaps with itself or even repeats and i wonder how you a-void-ed that when you were writing american monroe.

Well, I think that really covers it from this (bare) end.

I am threadbare, I am spooled out.

I don't know how I have gotten myself into something so much bigger than me.

Oh, there you are, ntalking me

That night we met on the Internet. For us it was not about romantic love, but a longing to connect. We simply wanted to have a good friendship. Now this is what I most savor. Loyalty and friendship are two of the most difficult things to maintain in this world. They are gifts I chose to embrace. When I encounter these rare graces in other human beings I am awestruck. The hardest thing is to keep believing, to keep caring, in the face of dissolution. When you are in the position of Job, it is easy to doubt, and even easier to give up. But I remember Job, and I know that he was able to believe in Grace even in the face of betrayal, loss, and what looked for a time to be the end of the world. *Hiroshima, Mon Amour*. The last gift I received from my father was a packet of postcards of the Hiroshima monument. He did not write on any of these cards. One sits on my desk as I write this. I see a solemn arch surrounded by flowers. I cannot read the description of the monument because the writing is in Japanese. But I treasure this packet of postcards as a reminder of the faith that endures even when living people are made into shadow-versions of themselves by an atomic blast. In later years others will remember, and they will keep building monuments and leaving flowers. Maybe they will buy a postcard. Postcards of the apocalypse now, but somehow I believe that a message can be sent and received and some form of faith may be retrieved.

So many people who want to believe, who want to find a true correspondent. How will they do this? I pick up the *Bay Guardian* and cruise the Personals section. I read a series of very specific requests for love and wonder if all those writing in should join I.A., or if maybe they have already joined and are stuck in "The Greek Way." Here are some of the ads I read, turned into broken-haikus of verse: loves sought, and bought and stolen and cursed. I read these ads and I cannot turn back. Found poetry, sad souls, written notes on the self: the personals ads that double as cries for help:

OLDER LADIES

25 year-old tall, dark and handsome European "love doctor" available for day and evening appointments. I have a sincere compassion for older, fuller-breasted ladies. All I ask is you be clean and discreet and sexy and I'll be discreet.

STRANGER TO FEELINGS

to explore for this WM curious about my submissive and masochistic side. I am careful, healthy, slim fit, romantic, and ready to be taught. I seek an attractive, dominant, and aggressive woman who is honest, healthy, and sincere. No professionals please.

MANIC-DEPRESSIVE?

I am a young male seeking a young M.D. nympho-female to indulge and explore consciousness and body. Race or weight unimportant. You are not crazy; you are awake, alive, and full of vitality. Share your prana with me.

TAKE ME TO BED

I'm slim, sexy, bi-curious, black hair, green-eyes, piercings. Sexually confident, exquisite kisser, lover, mistress, slave. Need uninhibited surrender—yours and mine. Straight and bi-sexual, sexy, long-haired, pierced, tattooed and/or dark-sided GQ pretty-boys—drown me in your masculinity. Breathtakingly gorgeous femmes desiring Anais Nin incarnate-dare.

TO THE WORLD

We are a nice, ordinary couple; bright, professional, refined. We're best of friends, financially secure, perhaps a bit aloof. But behind closed doors, I am your slave.

FEMINIST SUBMISSIVE?

I'm a dominant man who feels profoundly liberated by his relatively new take on sexuality. Your submission is a bases-clearing triple. You're a woman. 25–45. Smart above all, Romantic, successful A Feminist and a Femme Experience optional. Desire is not. I'm an artist, mid-30s easy to look at.

Did these people write the ads themselves, or did their friends help make them up? Who will answer them? Will a man arrive at their door with a box of letters and leave them messages of hope and love undying? Why are these notes posted in the paper? What are we all searching for? Do you want to answer any of these ads? Do you post your own ads in your local paper, or in a National Tabloid? What are we looking for here? Is it connection or disconnection? Is it all about making a connection, getting a love fix? Will love fix us? Writing to anonymous populations a nation types out advertisements for its selves and circulates them in the pages of the dailies: we live in imagined communities, we are all victims of our own imaginations. We play the role of victim in this imagined nation. Ah, Kerouac. Ahhhhhhh, Humanity. O, Norman Mailer. Sure, Marilyn Monroe.

Oh, Bartleby.

I open up a book I bought for a dollar called *Stage II Relationships: Love beyond Addiction*. The author is counseling those who have been addicts. Being addicted kept them from really connecting with their partners. Their connections have temporarily failed, but still the author has some hope for redemption. He gives the reader this advice:

No one is perfect, and there are no instant cures. Understand that whatever you ask of your partner, however small, may be difficult for your partner to give. Be patient in the presence of good intentions. If your partner is not living up to an agreement, but is

still trying, give him or her the benefit of the doubt. Don't make it
a crime to fail.

As we make contact across the net, trust is generated and
deepened. And trust is the name of the game.[42]

These words, so trite but true, are strangely moving this evening. Trust is the name of the game, the name game. The problem is how is one to trust in the faith of inevitable endings, corruption, petty-minded ways of being in the world? Is humanism being reborn for this author in the pages of a cheap self-help book? I don't know, but now where and whenever I can get words of encouragement I do so. And these words, however clichéd, offer some form of hope. This is not the Bible, but at least it is an attempt at faith. Can we learn to compromise, to be real to each other, to give each other the benefit of the doubt, even in the face of failure, of miscommunications, of breakdowns? I can simply say that I am trying. But in a virtual terrain this was no easy thing, and it works better for me mostly in daily life.

Virtual Democracy. We're all wired and tired. Don't read on me. This space for rent. Your face here. Don't hate me because I'm beautiful. I sing the body eclectic. I sing the tragedy, dyslexic. This is a dsylexIcon of meaning in our time. I will lay down this rap, but I'm part-time on line. I'm in the Vineland, tangled up in vines. I'm in the mind-land, trying to skip over mines. I'm Lewis Carroll, part-time over time. I'm Alice a lot, Cheshire-cat rose nine times. These are the lives that we lived at this stage. This is the theater that makes up the page.

People need to get out more often and talk to each other. Not on phones, not at conferences, not using computers, but on summer lawns moistened with the dew of the evening or is it the morning, lying on our backs and watching the clouds and reading poetry for no reason at all and drinking a nice Chardonnay and just sitting there. People who make you want to picnic are a blessing: do not overlook them in these tired times. It is good to be with someone; right there, to hold his or her hand, to kiss that cheek, to be silent or talking together in space. We all long for this in our own ways, twisted

42. Earnie Larsen,
Stage II Relation-
ships: Love beyond
Addiction (San
Francisco: Harper
SanFrancisco, 1987),
p. 89.

streets and sheets of grim intent and desire spell out so much of what it is we think we want when we want to *know*. We all want to know someone and for that person to know us. We are often afraid of being alone.

HINT: To KNOW other people is not to possess them. It is about letting them go; it is about seeing everything in them that is noble, and great, and stupid, and miraculous, and unique, and still caring, even knowing that you may never see them again, or that they may have no feelings for you. You can try and argue them into loving you but you'd do better off with a picnic or a conversation with someone who you know loves you. We should ask for simple gifts. Remember, the biggest part of the story is what is left out. In the end, there is no final accounting for ourselves and others. The loves we search hardest for are the loves we are most likely never to have had or to lose. We risk forms of self-addiction.

REPETITION

How beneficent a thunderstorm is! How blessed it is to be rebuked by God! As a rule, a person very easily becomes defiant when censured; when God judges, then he subsides, and, surrounded by the love that wishes to educate him, he forgets the pain.

Who could have imagined this ending? Yet no other ending is thinkable, and not this one, either. When everything has stalled, when thought is immobilized, when language is silent, when explanation returns home in despair—then there has to be a thunderstorm. Who can understand this? And yet who can conceive of anything else?[43]

43. Kierkegaard,
*Fear and Trembling /
Repetition*, p. 212.

THE WORLD WIDE WEB CASTS ITS NET AND BEGINS TO GIVE ME BACK MY FAMILY?

```
Date:     Tue, 30 Jul 1996 19:52:56 EDT
To:       S.Paige.Baty@williams.edu
From:     S.Paige.Baty@williams.edu
Subject:  Family Tree
```

> From: David Grant Baty <baty .nz>
>
> X-URL: http://www.williams.edu:803/PoliSci/baty/
>
> Hi,
>
> My name is David Baty, I was searching the WWW for other
> Batys to fill in time and came across your site.
>
> I live in New Zealand, having an unusual surname means there
> are few of us here. We have traced our decendant to a John Baty
> from England who arrived here in 1856.
>
> Anyway, I thought I would send a note.
>
> I live in a small city called Gisborne which is the first city to see
> the sunrise each day. I have a masters in tourism studies and my
> role here is to market Gisborne as the first city to welcome the
> New Millennium.
>
> I would be interested to hear more on the work you are
> currently undertaking.
>
> David Baty
> baty@voyager
>

Now, voyager, begin to unravel your family as we welcome in the New Millennium. Interestingly enough, he is not the first unknown relative to find me through the Internet, but that is another story and it does not take place in New England.—Paige

POST SCRIPT

Date: Fri, 16 Aug 1996 15:05:27 EDT
To: williams-faculty@williams.edu, williams-
          staff@williams.edu
From: @williams.edu
Subject: Physical Inventory of computer equipment

Return-Path: @williams.edu

Faculty and Staff,

We will be updating our physical inventory of our computer
systems on
campus and will be visiting your office shortly to check the
Williams
ID tag number on your computer. This will be done beginning
Monday
19-August and continue over the next 2 weeks, so do not be
alarmed if
you see someone looking at your computer. If you are not in your
office when we arrive, we will work through the departmental
secretary
or other appropriate person in order to gain access. We hope you
will
not mind us entering in your absence. It is important that we
verify
the accuracy of the College's computer inventory. The inventory
will
be done by students working for Technical Services for the
summer. They will identify themselves as representatives of the
Center
for Computing. We will try to inventory Faculty departments first
so
as not to disrupt the beginning of the semester.

We couldn't find you.

> @home, Paige.